From
BUST
to
BOOM

Ten Months Through the Eyes of a Bitcoiner

MARK HELFMAN

Introduction

From March 2020 to December 2020, I had a front row seat for bitcoin's crash from $8,000 to $3,800 and its subsequent boom to $31,000. In my newsletter, *Crypto is Easy*, I documented the crash, its aftermath, and bitcoin's long rise from the ashes of disaster.

Despite a global financial panic and pandemic disease, bitcoin blossomed in size, scope, and acceptance among mainstream investors. As a series of monthly newsletter posts for subscribers, this book chronicles bitcoin's journey—and my own—over those ten months.

Table of Contents

March 2020

Tough week for bitcoin.

[Note—bitcoin's price had started to crash from $8,000 to $3,800 when I published this issue.]

If you've read my free content, you know I expect up to two more years of higher prices. On the way up, we will have lots of horrible crashes. Fortunately, we also have some great data to tell us which crash is just a dip and which crash signals the end of the bull market.

(Yes, we are still in a bull market.)

Contrary to the news reports, bitcoin's price is not correlated with the U.S. stock market or any other financial asset. We have tons of evidence to prove that statement. Some weeks, prices move in tandem. Some weeks, they don't.

Despite epic crashes in traditional markets, we don't have any data suggesting this is the end of bitcoin's bull run. In fact, bitcoin's price can go as low as $5,400 *and still stay in a bull market.*

How Crypto Will Probably Evolve (and Why That Matters Now)

Do you know what's my biggest pet peeve about people's understanding of bitcoin?

They think of it only as money.

This narrow scope keeps people from appreciating the bigger picture: bitcoin is the unit of account for a peer-to-peer electronic cash system.

Over the years, that system—the blockchain, the network, the infrastructure built around it—has grown in size, scope, and value.

It's not *bitcoin* that gives this system its value. It's the other way around. *The system* gives bitcoin its value.

As that system grows, bitcoin will gain more value. Eventually, that system will serve as a global settlement layer for all sorts of transactions. When you exchange "things," you will use a product or service built on bitcoin's blockchain.

Few people will hold actual bitcoin in any quantity. They will continue to use local currencies, with APIs and merchant services converting their money in and out of bitcoin on demand. Only we and maybe 50 million other people will actually hold any significant amount of bitcoin.

(This is a very small number of people.)

A few altcoins will fill specific niches or support some unique product or service. You won't think about them as investments, just things you use to get what you want. E.g., you'll buy a little basic attention token (BAT) when you want to publish an ad. You won't expect to get rich, you just want to make sure a real person sees your ad.

In time, bitcoin's sidechains will replace many altcoins, but some alts will persist. Not only will they have loyal users and large networks, but they will offer something distinct and essential. People will not want to give them up without a compelling reason to switch to something else. That's human nature. We love convenient, familiar experiences that we can share with others.

So, maybe BAT will serve as the de facto currency for the internet while bitcoin does everything else, simply because that's what people get used to.

It'll take a while to get there, but once we do, the investment opportunity will disappear. That's why we need to stake our claims now.

Of course, that means we will have to wait longer to "get rich quick" and "win the lottery," as people say when they want to disparage the bitcoin OGs that bought in 2012 or 2015. We will also risk seeing some of our altcoins go to zero.

That's ok. We're playing for a stake in the financial networks of the future, not fast money from a fleeting bull run.

When we get to the peak of this market cycle, people will think we got lucky. In truth, we saw the opportunity before they did—and dared to put our money into it when nobody else would.

I recently posted my first video about the market right now, as well as my overall investment thesis. Here's the very short summary:

- My thesis: bitcoin makes a good investment because it's a hedge against the collapse of our financial system and its price tends to go up over time. So far, both statements remain true. Bitcoin's price has always stayed above the

200-week moving average, a mathematical formula that aggregates four years of investor behavior into a line on a chart. This line always goes up. Since price always stays above this line, and this line always goes up, we can assume this pattern will continue. Also, bitcoin's technology relies on math, not people. Math never fails. Computers will always do what they're programmed to do regardless of what's going on in the financial markets. Equations do not have counterparty risks.

- Today's market is in a very dangerous position but there's nothing to worry about *yet*. Ideally, we want to stay above $8,500. The longer we stay below that price, the more likely we're heading into a market shift that might push bitcoin's price down for a while. It's all related to the relationship of today's price with the 150-day moving average (150 DMA), a mathematical formula that tracks how prices have changed over the past 5 months.

- For bitcoin, the 150 DMA offers a very strong psychological signal about the overall market sentiment. When the price is above this line, people are generally positive. Momentum tends to carry bitcoin's price upwards. When the price is below this line, people are generally negative. Momentum tends to carry bitcoin's price downwards. Eventually, these trends shift as the 150 DMA catches up to the changes in price. The problem is, we can never know how long that will take. Let's hope we get above the 150 DMA (and stay there). As of today, the 150 DMA is slightly below $8,500.

- While I'm not worried yet, I would not assume this is "just a dip." That said, we are still in a bull market. Big drops happen *all the time* during bull markets. If you think a drop from $10,500 to $7,800 is bad, wait until we get a drop from $105,000 to $78,000. If we go where I think we're going to go, it will happen.

What's the difference between a bitcoin bull market and a bit-coin bear market?

In a bull market, the price sometimes goes up!

Relax and enjoy the ride!

April 2020

"There are decades where nothing happens, and there are weeks where decades happen."

We have had a few of those weeks. While the world's financial system teeters on the edge of collapse and deflationary depression, the cryptosphere is hyping bitcoin as a way to capitalize on the inflation from all the money governments are printing in response.

Talk about contrast.

I am not ready to look that far ahead.

First, the world's financial system needs to survive long enough for all that money to cause inflation. Then, bitcoin needs to survive long enough for the rest of the world to care about it.

Of all the things that keep me up at night, bitcoin is not one of them.

Do you know what really worries me?

Debt.

Namely, the collapse of debt markets. Read below for my thoughts on bitcoin, fiat, stocks, and debt markets.

Bitcoin: insulated from the chaos

Of all assets, bitcoin (and crypto as a whole) will probably suffer the least.

First, it's a tiny, insignificant market. At $100 billion, bitcoin's entire market cap is less than 1% of the S&P 500. Apple has enough cash on its books to buy every satoshi on earth (with money to spare).

Second, bitcoin's price movements are not correlated to those of any other assets. It does not move in sync with stocks, bonds, commodities, or other investment assets.

While some people say it's correlated to the stock market now, *there is no meaningful data* to suggest that. Correlation is a statistical concept, not something you can see from looking at lines on a chart. You can't compare six weeks of price movement and conclude it's correlated.

Did you know every warm day between March 1 - April 5, bitcoin's price went down? How's that for correlation? It's sunny and beautiful as I write this—CRASH COMING?!?!?!?

Third, almost nobody cares about bitcoin. From conversations I've had with people in the money management space, most "institutional investors" have put no money into the markets (yet). Of those that have any bitcoin, they've set aside a relatively small portion of their portfolios into it—enough to boost their portfolios if bitcoin succeeds, not enough to hurt their portfolios if it fails. Some of them undoubtedly sold a chunk of their position during the March 2020 crash, based on the research I showed you last month.

Fourth, bitcoiners tend to have more wealth and financial savvy than your average person. They're also younger, on average.

Many surveys and reports from exchanges show this. These are exactly the types of people who will suffer the least during the coming economic downturn.

When bitcoin's price dropped in March, exchanges saw a flood of new money coming in. Over the next weeks, that money moved to private wallets. As I mentioned in an earlier update, HODL waves showed bitcoins flowing from people who bought in late 2018 - early 2019 to new wallets and OG wallets.

This signals *strength*.

Thankfully, bitcoin is not a mainstream asset. It's insulated from the turbulence. But if it can weather this storm, it will prove it deserves a place in mainstream portfolios.

Fiat: demand for stablecoins will boost crypto

Also, the recent financial panic drove many people into stablecoins like USDT, DAI, USDC, etc. For example, USDC market cap went up 50% in March. USDT spiked 35% from $4.5 billion to $6 billion.

Do you know why my recent airdrop opportunity, Linen App, slashed its payout? Because Compound, the platform it supports, saw tons of money pour into it last month. Linen no longer needs to raise interest rates to attract U.S. depositors—people from all over the world are pouring capital into its platform without those extra incentives.

Why are people buying stablecoins?

Everybody wants dollars, and it's a lot easier for Asians and Africans to get USD-denominated stablecoins than actual dollars.

Also, some people prefer stablecoins. You can always access them—a nice assurance for anybody scared their banks will freeze withdrawals or fail outright.

While this stablecoin money has not flowed into bitcoin or alts yet, you can expect at least some of it will.

Stock market: not as big a deal as people think

Oddly enough, stocks do not correlate strongly to economic recessions and depressions. Sometimes, the stock market crashes before a recession, sometimes not. Sometimes the stock market booms during a recession, sometimes not.

Recessions come when production and revenue fall. In other words, when real business activity declines.

Stock markets do not reflect real business activity. Rather, they let investors speculate on the future success of the businesses that list on stock exchanges. Prices reflect confidence in the future.

Right now, according to people I know and the trade rags that cover financial markets, corporations have started selling shares and refinancing debt to include corporate assets like stock as collateral. While this should depress stock prices in the short-run, it's a good thing for the long-term health of the market.

Does this mean the stock market will rebound immediately? Corporations won't go out of business?

No. Stock prices will go down or stay roughly flat as businesses sell their shares into a weak market and investors stay on the sidelines.

You can expect investor confidence, corporate profits, and passive investment from workers to drop as the crisis deepens. How much and with what result?

Nobody really knows. "Expert" projections vary widely.

It's the overall financial situation, not the stock market itself, that you need to worry about.

Specifically, the debt markets.

Debt markets: worry now

Debt markets matter more than stock markets.

These complicated, opaque markets hold trillions of dollars of corporate, government, and household debt, plus all the derivative financial products based on that debt.

On top of about $100 trillion in government debt, the world has at least $200 trillion corporate and household debt, plus at least $400 trillion in financial products that depend on everybody repaying their IOUs.

It's a $700 trillion market.

(Possibly as much as $1 quadrillion.)

That's a lot of debt, and that's where the real trouble lies. China has an entire shadow banking system that's largely unregulated while Europe's banks have had trouble raising cash for a while.

While I will touch on some of that below, I'm going to focus mostly on the U.S. situation because it's what I know about. Besides, the U.S. financial system drives everything else. You need to know about it.

Here are the problems I see (btw this is not an exhaustive list).

Corporate debt

Many companies don't make enough money to pay their debts.

So-called zombie companies have used cheap credit to raise cash and buy-back their own stocks without boosting revenue. On the surface, this makes their balance sheet look ok. The problem is, without revenue, these companies can't survive without selling more equity or taking out more loans.

Now that economies have started shrinking, who's going to put money into these businesses? Why would banks and investors put money into a crappy business that can't make money instead of a business that's lean and primed for growth? Even if they wanted to do so, where will that money come from?

If you're really wonky, read "LEVERAGED LENDING AND CORPORATE BORROWING: Increased Reliance on Capital Markets, With Important Bank Links." This report from U.S. FDIC, the quasi-governmental entity that insures bank deposits, warned about excessive corporate debt months ago.

Essentially, we have lots of big corporations with worse finances than your average start-up firm—lots of debt and cash but not enough revenue to survive without somebody else pumping money into them.

Now, nobody wants to pump money into them.

[Note—shortly after I wrote this, the U.S. government pumped money into them.]

Banks running out of money

Banks occasionally end the day short on cash. When this happens, the U.S. Federal Reserve lends them money to balance the books and settle their accounts. The banks send the money back to the Fed the next day.

Normally, this is no worry. Banks have money coming and going all the time, it's impossible for every bank to always have enough money to settle every account.

BUT

Last year, the Fed opened a $400 billion lifeline to banks that fell short of their daily balance requirements. That's a lot of money. AND it was an open-ended program.

So, either lots of small banks or one/two large banks ran out of money.

Yes, that's right. *RAN OUT OF MONEY.*

That is the only reason for the Fed to keep this lifeline so large and open-ended. As I asked on Twitter for months, why are banks running out of money after ten years of economic boom and record profits?

The Fed still has that lifeline open, with one change.

Instead of capping the lifeline at $400 billion, *it removed all limits.*

Last week, a West Virginia bank failed. How many more will follow?

Commercial rents drying up

With so many businesses on lockdown across the world, commercial landlords have had a terrible time collecting rent. They need this rent to pay their mortgages and construction loans, as well as any other financing for which their property is collateral.

(On top of their normal expenses.)

Without rent, commercial landlords can't pay their lenders. As a result, the lenders can't recycle their payments into new loans.

Credit markets have already started to freeze.

Not good.

Sovereign debt markets still out-of-whack

Every big government has record budget deficits. It's been this way for a long time, but for the most part, those debts followed a rational pattern: governments issue debt, investors buy debt, governments settle those debts, investors make money, investors buy more debt.

This system works because investors mostly believe governments will not default on their debts *and* many countries have grown fast enough to justify that belief. It's why all the major economies can borrow essentially at-will—they only have to worry about losing investors to other countries that offer more attractive rates.

Last year, that whole dynamic changed.

Globally, negative-yield bonds reached a mind-boggling $15 trillion. Investors essentially paid governments to hold their money.

In October, U.S. treasuries saw an inverted yield curve, which suggests investors wanted to pay more for riskier, long-term debt than safer, short-term debt.

To boot, the U.S. Federal Reserve recently promised to backstop foreign debt defaults. This signals at least one G7 country is worried it will default on its debt, or perhaps the G7 countries worry about a default by some other big country with large debt obligations to the G7.

On March 25, 2020, rates on short-term U.S. government debt briefly dropped below zero. Investors worried so much about the value of other governments' bonds that they took short-term losses to avoid exposing their wealth to foreign governments' debt.

Now, Southern European countries have started negotiating with Northern European countries on new "Coronavirus bonds." Why do Italy, Spain, and the rest of the south need their northern neighbors to cosign their loans? If Northern European countries really believe Italy and Spain can repay their debts, why don't they sign on?

None of this is normal.

Derivatives at risk of margin calls

In normal times, derivatives hedge risks. They're a form of market insurance, though some traders use them as speculative investment vehicles.

Often, businesses and traders borrow money to buy derivatives using margin accounts, a sort of credit account. As a result, they can cover the risks of market disruption or price spikes/crashes without spending too much money.

As long as the prices of the underlying assets stay reasonably predictable, this isn't a problem. For massively volatile assets, volatility gets priced in. For stable assets, stability gets priced in.

When markets went crazy last month, it sent the whole system off-kilter. Normal valuations fell apart. As a result, many businesses and traders could not cover shortfalls in their margin accounts. They had to either raise cash or sell their assets. Some analysts speculate these margin calls led to last month's near-universal sell-off in literally every investment asset except U.S. dollars.

If this financial crunch continues, even "safe" assets like bonds, collateralized debt, and maybe even USD will get crushed as borrowers are forced to sell their positions to cover their loans.

Very bad.

Mortgages next?

Up to this point, the residential mortgage industry has not felt any ill-effects, at least in the U.S.—but everybody expects it will soon.

When homeowners lose their jobs and businesses, they can't pay their mortgages. When renters lose their jobs and businesses, they can't pay rent to their landlords, many of whom have their own mortgages (and lots of other costs involved in residential property management).

On top of that, real estate finance is incredibly complicated with many moving parts. For example, the Fed can bail out borrowers but mortgage companies would still be on the hook for making payments to investors who hold mortgage-backed securities. Propping up one part of the market could destroy another part of the market. It's very vulnerable to butterfly effects.

U.S. government has taken extreme measures to backstop the mortgage industry with pass-through assistance, a new forbearance program, and a scheme to advance servicers the cost of missing payments.

Is it enough? Can the Fed implement these programs in a way that balances all the competing financial needs of all the different players?

We'll see. My mortgage broker tells me lenders have started pulling out of some of these programs because they expect a wave of foreclosures this year . . .

Emerging markets on edge

Many developing countries, aka emerging markets, depend on Chinese investment and debt denominated in U.S. dollars.

Why would they take Chinese investment?

Because China gives them a sweet deal, often building infrastructure and technology at little or no cost. In return, China asks for their loyalty and favorable trade policies.

Why do they repay their debts in U.S. dollars?

Because their creditors demand it. Investors worry emerging market currencies will lose too much of their value, but never worry about the value of the U.S. dollar.

This explanation simplifies a more complicated situation, but it's good enough for this post.

Why does this matter?

As the dollar rises in value, these countries find it harder to repay their debts. It costs them more of their own currency to buy dollars. As a result, they need to either make more money or sell more dollar-denominated goods like corn, oil, soybeans, etc.

You can see the problem, right?

If they all spend their currency for dollars, that will raise the price of the dollar while depleting their currency reserves. As a result, they will need even more of their own currency to buy more dollars at a higher price—and where will they get more money?

They could raise taxes and implement austerity programs, but these things will crush their economy and make their people really mad.

Alternatively, they could also simply print more money, but perpetuates the downward spiral. This approach led Germany to hyperinflation after WWI (its debt was denominated in gold not dollars, but with the same effect).

In other words, they have to either kill their economy or inflate their money out of existence.

Why don't these developing nations produce more goods denominated in dollars or export more products intended for U.S. markets?

Because they worry about how China will respond. Besides, what happens if the U.S. uses tariffs and trade restrictions to shut foreign goods out of U.S. markets?

Hope and prayers

We don't know how significant or extreme any of these problems are.

While all these problems have solutions, implementing and coordinating them is a delicate balancing act. Walking the tight rope.

Central banks are bailing out everybody they can while governments throw money at people. It's all designed to keep the world's economies afloat while everybody ramps up medical countermeasures to Coronavirus.

Somebody called this nationalizing the financial markets.

That's basically what's going on—governments and central banks are using public funds to buy trillions of dollars of debt and rig the markets until humanity has the capacity to treat people infected with COVID-19.

While this creates all sorts of moral hazards and unintended consequences, consider the alternative: pandemic disease, financial ruin, and widespread death all at once. At least with this intervention, they stand a chance of tackling each crisis one at a time.

The question now is what comes first: a collapse of the debt markets or the end of the pandemic.

Let's hope for the latter and pray that when the time comes, we can all recover.

How this relates to bitcoin

The global financial system is having a heart attack. It doesn't have enough money to pay for the surgery. Governments have agreed to save the patient now, then deal with the money problems later.

Meanwhile, everybody will suffer. You, me, and those we love. Every asset will see volatility in the coming months. Bailouts and defaults will make people really, really mad. At least one government will probably need IMF intervention. China or Italy might implode (hopefully not). It will get worse before it gets better.

Worse than 2008? Worse than 1929? Worse than 1873?

I wish I knew. There's no reason to believe things have to get that bad or last that long. Even if some things go wrong, the world's financial systems will probably be ok (mostly).

We just need to HODL tight, use bitcoin as we need to, and stack a few sats when we have money to spare. Bitcoin might serve as the backbone for a new financial system that doesn't depend on any of the things people will grow to hate over the next year or two (namely, governments, banks, corporations). DeFi and payment platforms may soon have their time in the sun.

They're not ready yet, but they'll have to be.

Tough times all around right now. Of all the things to worry about, worry about your friends, your family, and yourself.

When it comes to bitcoin, relax and enjoy the ride.

May 2020

Happy halving, everybody.

This is the third issue of Crypto is Easy. It's pretty long but I have a lot to say! If it seems like too much, follow me on Medium and Twitter. I'll break this update into smaller bits of content, probably with some elaboration, that I'll publish over the next few weeks on different platforms.

As *CIE* subs, you get the whole thing one post—before everybody else does.

In this issue, I'll talk a little about bitcoin and altcoins, and finish with a larger discussion about the global financial situation and why too many people are getting ahead of themselves.

Mindset is everything now

I know some of you may have gotten a little spooked by the 20% drop in bitcoin's price since Thursday. Right now, bitcoin's price is $8,600.

These types of swings should not matter. If this really is the start of that big bull market everybody thinks it is, you're going to see many, many more swings of 20% over three days. Sometimes, you will get a 20% drop in one day.

On the flip side, you will have times when the price goes up and you feel like you have to buy more. Like it's getting away from you and will never come back.

You might already have felt that sensation when we popped over $8,000 at the end of last month. Maybe you were kicking yourself that you didn't buy more when bitcoin's price crashed, like you missed the boat or you made a mistake.

You can't think that way.

Yeah, if you've followed my plan for bitcoin's bull market since I posted it on March 30, 2020, you would've bought bitcoin between $5,400 and $7,800. My earliest readers know I picked up some more bitcoin during and right after that big crash in March—*despite worrying that price would keep going lower and preparing to exit the market.*

It's natural to fear missing out. Even more natural to fear losing money.

To really make the most of this bull market, you need to act in spite of your fears. Courage is not the absence of fear, but the ability to act in spite of it.

Stay courageous.

So . . . do we buy now?

If you want to dollar cost average, you're going to do great. My plan will do better, but if you follow it perfectly, you will go for long periods of time without buying. With dollar-cost averaging, you can always feel like you're getting a piece of the action without taking much risk.

Like they say about poker, bitcoin is a whole lot of boredom punctuated by moments of terror and ecstasy.

That said, *it is never a bad time to buy bitcoin.*

Just keep in mind, bitcoin's price can crash from any price at any time. The higher it goes, the more likely it will crash. You don't want to wait until the price goes way up.

What's *my* goal?

Ride this thing up, buy at the very best opportunities, and sell before all those greedy people, HODLERS, and fake maximalists sell out and crash the market.

If we NEVER sell, all the better. That means bitcoin will have succeeded.

Altcoins?

As for altcoins, they're *all* speculative, even Ethereum and XRP, and they tend to move in the same direction as bitcoin, so I don't follow their prices. These long-term plays will take years to develop. Many will die along the way.

Except for Chainlink, none of the big ones interest me and there are way too many small ones to cover.

[Note—with the subsequent movement of altcoins into the top 10, I now have several big altcoins that interest me at the top.]

That said, I'm starting a list. Send me any alts you want me to look into.

Several people have asked for my portfolio or recommendations—I hear you. One day, I may share.

Why don't I post more often?

Time.

I will always keep you informed when the markets move in a way that might affect my plan or if there's something going on that I feel like you should be thinking about. Right now, there's no action, we're waiting for the dip.

A real dip, not one of those 20% drops like the one we just had, those moves that send Twitter in a frenzy. I'm looking for those 30-40% crashes that we should see 6 or 7 times before we get to the market cycle peak.

Make sure you're subscribed to my YouTube channel. I plan to better utilize that outlet, rather than spam your inbox.

You can also follow me on Medium and Twitter, where I post content about how cryptocurrency and blockchain technology will change the world. CIE focuses more on what's going on with the markets, looking at the big picture rather than the daily news.

Why we stick to the big picture

To really make the best decisions, you have to understand what's going on around you—that larger world of which crypto is a small part. If you focus only on what's in front you, only the day-to-day, you will not see the opportunities lying well ahead. You'll worry about things that can easily change and neglect the things that can't. You'll assume a problem is permanent when it's temporary and assume temporary problems are permanent.

I do this. We all do this.

Like, for example, the people who bought oil contracts and silver in April.

Silver plays no role in modern finance and we have enough oil above ground to last six months *under normal economic conditions,* far longer if economies remain shut down.

Over that same time period, those same people also bought stocks of companies that have no customers or revenue.

Yet these are the same people who think we're crazy for buying bitcoin.

Perception is reality

My political science professor once told me "where you stand depends on where you sit."

We all come to the world with our own biases, usually trying to justify our gut decisions with some sort of logic or rationale. Our beliefs make us take a certain position. Our circumstances make us seek a certain outcome.

At this moment, you see a lot of contradictory statements from mainstream economists, financial analysts, and everybody else. The cryptosphere has lots of people who have only a very basic understanding of how markets work, but they all seem very confident in their opinions.

Each of these people has a certain viewpoint. They may or may not be right.

Some look at crumbling financial markets and a big drop in economic activity, combined with massive government intervention, and conclude we're going to get hyper-inflation and a global depression.

Others look at crumbling financial markets and a big drop in economic activity, combined with massive government intervention, and conclude we're going to get a modest recession and V- or U-shaped recovery.

They can't both be right.

Prepare for a great depression or a mild downturn?

As fearful as people might get about the horrific economic data, there's no reason the world has to fall apart.

Possible?

Of course. So many people have lost jobs and businesses over the past two months. Economic output has fallen off a cliff. Some national currencies have already crumbled. It's hard to imagine we'll ever recover.

Keep in mind, those big, deep, long-lasting financial crises do not come from short-term downturns in economic activity, even if those drops are significant. People are resilient and economies tend to adjust more quickly than you'd think.

Those devastating, multiyear, civilization-threatening collapses happen when "safe" assets lose their value quickly.

Why?

Because in modern economies, safe assets form the basis of all financial activities. Households, businesses, and governments create all sorts of financial arrangements based on an assumption of low risk. Countries build economies on that assumption. Banks and financiers do trillions of dollars in business on that assumption.

When that assumption fails, everything else does.

There's a reason crashing oil prices don't threaten the global financial system. People know it's risky and volatile. They factor that into their decisions. *Nobody* will ever pool oil contracts into collateralized loan obligations. Mortgages? No problem.

Safe assets, not risky assets, screw everything up.

In 2008, it was U.S. houses. In 1929, it was U.S. and British stocks. In 1873, it was railroads and gold.

At the time, people saw these assets as sure bets, assets that could never crash. When they did, all hell broke loose.

Outside of those three events, we have had many economic downturns and plenty of regional financial crises. Terrible events that *nobody* should ever want to live through, but none of them destroyed the global economic order.

You can have pain, hardship, and turmoil without systemic failure. People suffer, then recover. Life goes on.

In fact, most economic pullbacks last about a year or less, but most of the world's largest economies haven't seen that type of pullback in a decade or more. And *none* of those pullbacks were confronted with a massive, coordinated intervention *at the beginning.*

Choose your history wisely

Twitter obsesses over 2008 and 1929, but I'd like to highlight one other historical event that's worth noting.

In 1948, the U.S. economy went negative. At the time, many feared the country would have a new Great Depression.

Instead, they got a one-year recession. Really bad, but not the economic carnage most people predicted at the time.

How much of those fears came from people's mindset, rather than the actual reality of what was going on? How much of today's fears come from a similar mindset?

Back then, the U.S. had not seen a major economic downturn since 1937. That was over a decade prior and it came when the U.S. thought it had finally recovered from the 1929 crash. For most people, that 1937 dip was their most recent memory of a bad economy. For some, it was their *only* memory.

For us, our most recent memory is the 2008 financial disaster and the European debt crisis that followed. That was over a decade ago, and it came when the U.S. thought it had finally recovered from the dot-com crash and 9/11 attacks.

Could we be psyching ourselves out like everybody did in 1948?

I'm not saying we *won't* get a new great depression. I'm saying *we don't have to* get one.

Yes, national currencies could go haywire, wars could break out, and lots of horrible things could happen. The world can change at any moment.

But you can say that any time.

As I wrote in last month's issue, some countries could default on their sovereign debts. Other "safe" assets could fail, too.

If that happens, all bets are off. Things would get really ugly, really quickly.

We have lots of people working hard to make sure that doesn't happen. How do you know they won't succeed?

Unemployment—bad, but not predictive

When 25% of your country loses their jobs in two months, like the U.S. just did, you should panic. I can't imagine worse news, nor what it must feel like for people suddenly out of work.

People talk about the unemployment during the Great Depression, but it took *three years* for unemployment rate to peak. Once it did, the economy recovered.

According to The Balance, unemployment rose 8% to 16% to 24% from 1930-1932, then fell steadily for the next decade.

We are already at the Great Depression peak. Does that mean will see unemployment triple over the next three years, as it did at the start of the Great Depression? We will get 70% unemployment?

Unfortunately, it's possible, but who's to say that *has to* happen? We already hit the same peak as we did in 1932 when the employment rate started to improve. Why can't that happen this time?

Historically, unemployment *leads* recessions and recoveries. The rate hits bottom right before a downturn, then peaks after the economy recovers.

It's an inverse correlation, as shown in this chart from Macrotrends:

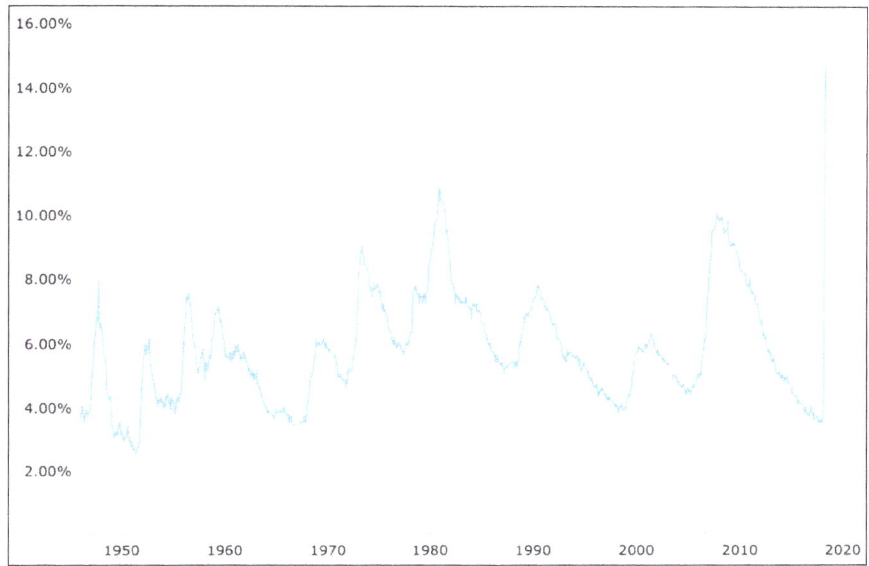

Low unemployment often masks underlying problems, like U.S. real wages flat since 2017, U.S. manufacturing in a recession since 2019, U.S. banks short on capital for months, and falling retirement contributions among U.S. workers for years—before coronavirus was even a thing.

Recovery happens in spite of high unemployment.

But trends sometimes end. Our present situation is unprecedented. Very, very scary. I worry about it all the time.

Think out of both sides of your head

As scary as the present is, remember the future is full of possibilities, not certainties.

Your doctor prescribes Tylenol because, in the past, it reduced fevers in almost every person who took it. Sometimes, it doesn't work. Does that mean you should not listen to your doctor?

No, it just means life doesn't always turn out like you expect, even if data and common sense seem to predict a certain outcome.

For example, almost *everybody* believes the U.S. real estate market will drop. After all, nobody's buying, everybody's losing their jobs, lenders keep dropping out of federal programs, forbearances have skyrocketed, renters are skipping out, and banks are bracing for a wave of foreclosures.

So why have my property values gone up 5% since the beginning of March? I would expect to see 5% gains in a normal year. To do so in six weeks is pretty significant.

Why would prices go up in the midst of crashing financial markets and pandemic disease? When nobody's touring houses and lenders are cutting back on loans? When the entire market is in a sort of stasis and fear?

Wall Street Journal says new home listings plummeted.

What happens if that trend continues? If people decide to stay in the house they own? If they recently refinanced to a low rate they might lose if they move? If their employer extends telework so they don't feel the need to move for work? If empty nesters let their unemployed kids move back home instead of downsizing? If retirees delay the purchase of that condo? If renters go back to work and make enough to cover rent again? If they don't and the government keeps paying their rent?

If that happens, the supply of available houses will shrink. They may not keep up with demand—even if both fall. Combine that with all this new money the Fed is throwing around, we might see real estate prices continue to go up.

Or not.

If trained, highly-educated experts with decades of experience can't predict the outcome, what makes you think you or I can?

You don't like central banks. You need them.

The European Central Bank has spawned so many memes over the years, I can understand why people think it's a laughing stock. Central banks in general get a bad rap.

Do you realize they're the biggest source of stability for the world's financial markets? That our modern complacency stems from central banks doing *too good* of a job at keeping the system moving?

I realize some of you live in Europe. For this section, I hope you'll indulge me in a discussion of the U.S. intervention. As the U.S. remains the largest single economy on earth, this intervention essentially puts the world at the mercy of the U.S. government.

(Sorry about that. Not my fault!)

Since the 2008 financial crisis, the Fed has developed the infrastructure and authority to buy out all sorts of debt. As part of its coronavirus relief package, U.S. Congress expanded those authorities and created a bunch of new government programs.

For an example of how these programs work, take the Main Street Lending Program. Small businesses can get loans of up to four years and $25 million. The Fed buys 95% of the loan from the bank, leaving the bank at risk for just 5% of the loan value. Banks, of course, get to collect a small fee from the Fed for participating.

In other words, the Fed is paying banks to make bad loans to businesses that will fail.

This is an Austrian economist's worst nightmare. It's also exactly the kind of thing your average person finds really shady.

Of course, if you own the business getting that bailout loan, you probably feel differently. If your job depends on that business, you *definitely* feel differently.

And for everybody else who lives in an economy that thrives on businesses staying open and people paying their bills, you need the intervention.

You have to weigh those moral hazards and market risks against the hazards and risks of a global financial meltdown. Thanks to coronavirus, the world lost about 5% of its GDP—and that's just the start.

How do you make up all that loss?

You can't.

But you can try to staunch the bleeding before the patient dies, in the hopes the patient can recover. No doctor would refrain from giving the Heimlich because he or she doesn't want to "reward" another person for careless eating.

What else needs a bailout?

Municipal bonds, corporate debt, auto loans, mortgages, you can run down the list. Messari already did, and it's a lot to scroll through.

I'm certain our central bankers understand the political and economic risks of their actions. I very much doubt they want to nationalize the debt markets.

What's the alternative? Let everything fall apart?

In 2008, the Fed bought out lots of debt (albeit six months too late). By 2014, it had unwound all those bad loans and undone all those drastic actions.

Who's to say it can't do that again?

But inflation!

Inflation is not bad.

That's a taboo thing to say in the bitcoin community, but it's true.

A little inflation encourages lending, investment, and economic activity. When money holds its value, people don't want to spend it. You need people to spend money to keep the economy growing.

Inflation helps asset holders and people with fixed debt arrangements. As they gain equity, they can pay off debt, borrow with more collateral, or sell assets for more money. Those gains move into the financial pipeline or get spent on goods and services. This money either recirculates to other people or boosts the value of property.

The problem is, inflation destroys the value of labor and savings. Your work and money continually lose value over time. As a result, it gets harder and harder to keep up, much less get ahead.

That's why inflation is sometimes called a stealth tax.

Most people have only their work and their money. If they own a house, it's the only asset that benefits from inflation—but barely, once you consider the taxes, mortgage costs, and maintenance expenses. Of those who have some retirement investments, most don't have enough to really matter.

In other words, inflation helps the few at the cost of the many.

The solution is to own assets that produce value. That way, you benefit from inflation. Your property will go up. Your debts will be easier to pay. Your businesses will generate more cashflow.

While you may not gain *purchasing power* as your money loses value, you do gain wealth from your productive assets. As long as people don't have an alternative source of money OR inflation happens slowly enough they don't realize, governments can inflate money forever.

Bitcoin is that alternative source of money that will protect you from inflation.

But, negative yields!

Negative yields don't make sense. They're not sustainable.

At least, I used to think so . . .

As long as investors continue to believe governments will pay back their debts, investors will continue to lend money to them—even at negative interest rates.

Some legitimately believe in the safety and security of sovereign debt. Some buy expecting to sell when rates go even more negative. Some (like me) use them to counterbalance other investments as part of a diversified portfolio.

On the flip side, central banks control how much these bonds are worth. While they can't change the number printed on the bond note, they can reduce its value through inflation and devaluation.

A lot of people think this is a bad thing.

Bitcoin doesn't care—it's programmed to gain value as long as people use it. Nobody can devalue bitcoin.

But, who will pay!

We will all pay.

But that would happen whether or not governments intervened. How would you like your suffering—deep, sudden, and widespread or shallow, lengthy, and contained?

What if all this government spending is not enough? Worse, what if it can't get into the hands of the people who need it, quickly, in the way you need it to?

For example, take one fairly small program, the U.S. government's Paycheck Protection Program (PPP). Designed as risk-free loans for small businesses to cover payroll costs, the initial $349 billion in funds ran out in just 13 days.

While the news raged about the 0.2% of funds that went to huge, publicly traded companies, nobody realized 95% of small businesses did not get *any* money from the program.

U.S. Congress has approved another $310 billion in funds for the PPP program.

It's not enough.

Eventually, money runs out, even if you can conjure it up at will. At some point, you need real economic activity to get that money flowing around the economy, get those debt markets back in shape, and generate real profits and new wealth.

Each new program makes it harder and harder to get that *healthy* economic activity.

All the worse when some of the beneficiaries use loopholes to pocket their bailout money at the public's expense.

Bitcoin doesn't have loopholes.

Re-opening the economy will not work

Some say reopening the economy will get everything back to normal.

These people do not understand how pandemic disease works, nor how humans respond to pandemic disease.

No matter what rules you set on social distancing, movement, and worker/customer safety, we will see more infections, hospitalizations, and deaths as economies reopen. It may also freak people out as they see more of their friends, family, and coworkers dead, dying, and permanently disabled over the coming months.

While many people think reopening the economy will get it back to normal, I am not one of them.

Many workers will not want to go back to dangerous jobs (especially in the U.S., because they have another 2-3 months of unemployment benefits to tide them over). Many people will not want to go to restaurants and public events knowing they could catch COVID-19.

Without any intervention, you will see more sick workers calling out, more experienced leaders dying, more disruptions to factories and supply chains simply from people catching COVID-19 on a massive scale. This will drag economies as much, possibly more, than lockdown.

Some people in the U.S. point to Sweden as a model for keeping the economy open while dealing with coronavirus. Sweden's own central bank predicts its economy will lose 7-10% GDP, among the worst of all developed nations. Meanwhile, its death rate is among the highest. Its own coronavirus chief told the press almost every part of the Swedish response failed.

Not the model I would want to follow.

True, the world has ramped up the production of medical supplies, tests, and personal protective equipment while accelerating vaccine development and disease tracking. We are learning more about the disease with every passing day. Our capacity to handle the disease in May 2020 is much better than it was in January 2020.

This lulls people into a false sense of security. Yes, lockdown is hard. Yes, most people who get COVID-19 are fine. Losing your job and business is terrible. Everybody wants to get back to normal.

On the other hand, this disease spreads as easily as the common cold and kills 10-20x more efficiently than the flu. Despite lockdowns, social distancing, and massive ramp-up of medical countermeasures, more than 60,000 people have died in the U.S. over the past two months. That's already more than all flu deaths over the past SIX months.

If you take the middle range of estimate of mortality, which is just the middle of all the (very wide-ranging) estimates I've seen, we should expect about 500,000 Americans will die from coronavirus this year. That's the same death rate as cancer (0.15%).

In reality, that number should go much higher because COVID-19 spreads so quickly and seems to reinfect people at a much higher rate than other infectious diseases.

I suspect everybody will change their tune as more people suffer from the virus, more hospitals close from the financial strain of treating mass casualties, and more parts of the workforce get sick or hospitalized.

At that point, it will be too late.

I don't know if reopening is going to be *worse* for the economy than staying shut. People with drug addictions and mental health issues have had a terrible time with the lockdown. Lots of businesses are on the brink of closing (if they haven't already gone out of business).

And, people need to work.

I'm sure the idea that it'll all be over and we'll get back to normal and the economy will recover, that's part of the thinking that goes into a lot of the decisions people are making now.

If anybody thinks that everything will be better in a few months, they're probably going to discover a different reality.

People pin their hopes on a vaccine, but that will take a while and may not end up very effective. Once we can test and trace everybody, then isolate all people at risk, we can really get the economy moving—but we don't have enough tests and besides, do you really think voters will go along with that?

Government crypto to the rescue?

You may have heard that Congressional Democrats tried to use the coronavirus relief package to get the U.S. central bank to create a digital dollar. That would make the U.S. the third country to digitize its national cryptocurrency, after China and The Marshall Islands.

Does that mean the U.S. government wants cryptocurrency?

No, but it does mean cryptocurrency has gained legitimacy among some policymakers.

Members of Congress have introduced 32 crypto bills since 2019. Almost half of them tell the government to investigate terrorism, money laundering, and trafficking of humans and drugs.

Does this mean Congress thinks cryptocurrency is for terrorists, sex traffickers, drug dealers, and money launderers?

No, but it does mean those are Congress's biggest concerns right now.

I would not read anything more into it. Congress is largely clueless about all this stuff.

With enough education and persistent lobbying, they'll come around. Unless bitcoin goes to $100k or China's blockchain poses serious competition with the U.S. dollar, cryptocurrency will remain at the bottom of the legislative priority list.

Don't underestimate the chances of that happening, though. Facebook published a whitepaper and the U.S. government flipped its wig. We got emergency hearings and a Presidential statement.

All that from a press release.

It doesn't take much to get politicians to act when there are votes and money at stake.

Speaking of Facebook . . .

When Facebook first announced its plans to create the Libra cryptocurrency, I loved the idea.

(Not Facebook, but the idea of a corporate cryptocurrency.)

After relentless pressure from governments, Libra Association watered down the project. It's no longer a game-changing, paradigm-shifting effort that will challenge long-held notions of privacy and monetary sovereignty.

It's just another way for a centralized entity to move money from one customer to another.

Libra will no longer be permissionless and will have comprehensive anti-money laundering protocols. It will allow law enforcement to see personal transactions and enable countries to enforce sanctions over coins in the network.

It will also give users stablecoins denominated in their local currency, rather than an independent currency backed by a basket of financial assets.

Why do they even bother with blockchain?

Score: Government money monopoly 1, people 0.

China leads again

As mentioned earlier, China continues to push forward with its central bank digital currency and plans to launch its Blockchain Service Network (BSN), dubbed "the blockchain of blockchains."

You can imagine my surprise when I read that BSN will connect with public blockchains like Ethereum and bitcoin. If that's true, every person in China will soon have only one degree of separation between the yuan and bitcoin, as well as a framework for using cryptocurrency as part of their normal, daily lives.

And you wonder when we'll get mass adoption?

I doubt a billion Chinese citizens will all suddenly buy bitcoin. China will control every aspect of BSN, undoubtedly blocking swaps of yuan with any currency, national or digital.

But you never know, right? If the Communist Party thinks pumping bitcoin's price will undermine the U.S. dollar, they just might loosen the reigns. Or perhaps their developers will create exclusive linkages with Party-sanctioned blockchains that trade publicly.

Even if that doesn't happen, BSN will give cryptocurrency a greater sense of legitimacy—or better yet, *inevitability*.

When doing research for a series of posts about conversations we have about crypto, one person said the most effective argument he's made is "this is the way everything's going."

The inevitability of cryptocurrency is a very powerful argument.

Also, don't discount the potential for China's digital yuan to get other countries to do the same with their own currencies. In a post-bailout world, voters may like the idea of a national currency that their governments can send directly to their wallets rather than to the banks and financiers.

India catching up?

Around the same time the coronavirus pandemic crashed financial markets, the Supreme Court of India overturned the country-wide banking ban against crypto.

According to <u>Coindesk</u>, Indian exchanges saw massive new volume soon after the announcement.

From my contacts in India, people *really* worry that banks will run out of money and the government will confiscate their wealth.

Cryptocurrency solves that problem. You can expect people will use it.

So, we now have the two biggest countries on earth with better access to cryptocurrency than ever before, just as prices are starting to rebound and people are losing faith in traditional assets.

Buy the substance, not the hype

If it seems like the stars are aligning for cryptocurrency, you may be right. But let's not get too far ahead of ourselves.

We can all be victims of our own mindset.

When your mindset is governments are bad, fiat money is bad, and people and government are not worthy of your trust, then times like these are going to skew your expectations in favor of bitcoin.

While everybody else is hyping the halving and BRRR memes, I like to dig a little deeper so you can make the best decisions about bitcoin and altcoins, rather than buying into the hype.

When I got into crypto in late 2017, I bought into every "mainstream" narrative. Chinese New Year. U.S. tax season. $6k is the bottom. Bakkt. China. Halving.

Some of those terms may not make sense to you if you're new. They're just excuses people used to explain the ups and downs of bitcoin's price and the wider market.

People get wrapped up in these stories, but bitcoin's simply a computer code. Everybody else turned it into digital gold and a store of value and the coin of freedom and whatever else they think it is.

Satoshi modeled some aspects of bitcoin around gold because it helped him explain the concept of miners and scarcity.

In fact, the word "gold" appears in only one sentence of the bitcoin white paper:

"The steady addition of a constant amount of new coins is analogous to gold miners expending resources to add gold to circulation."

Bitcoin is not gold. Its price and behavior have no correlation to anything that happens in the traditional financial markets. Its code works under all economic conditions. Its network continues to grow. Its development community continues to expand.

That is all that matters.

For that reason, I stick to an investment thesis, rather than a narrative. Otherwise, it's too easy to get lost in the moment. It's too easy to lose perspective.

My thesis?

As an investment asset, bitcoin serves as a hedge against the collapse of the traditional financial system. Also, its price goes up over time.

Plus, you can send bitcoin to anybody, anywhere, anytime, in any amount, instantly, without ever taking a single bit of personal information about the other person. No other technology can do that. Not a reason to invest, but a nice perk!

Money for everybody

Best of all, *bitcoin is accessible.* Anybody can get it and use it.

Unlike most assets, you can buy a tiny bit of bitcoin. You can keep buying a little bit more and a little bit more. You don't need permission, just a willing seller.

You also have a lot of guys like me who can look inside the market because of the transparency of bitcoin's blockchain, as opposed to digging through corporate quarterly reports and financial statements that hide everything bad unless the people in charge think they'll get sued or jailed for hiding the truth.

Bitcoin is public, open, and anybody can claim a small stake in its network. That has massive social value regardless of anything going on in the real world.

It's rare to find an asset of any kind that anybody can buy and use at any time. And it's crazy to think that only you, me, and a small number of other people realize this.

Over the next few years, many more people will realize this.

China and India matter not because they have people and money, but because *it's easy for their people to move their money into bitcoin and other cryptocurrencies.*

Does that mean bitcoin's price will explode?

Probably, but maybe not. Anybody can create a money system that's better than bitcoin. Some altcoins may have already done so.

Also, don't be so sure that people in the traditional financial world won't get their shit together, or that the world's financial leaders won't regulate cryptocurrency in a way that destroys its special role.

If you don't know what I mean by that, read my book, *Bitcoin or Bust: Wall Street's Entry Into Cryptocurrency.*

Stay diversified

That's why it's important to stay diversified, not just in your investments but also in your mindset. Think out of both sides of your head. Set realistic expectations, plan for one outcome, prepare for another.

It's tempting to want to put as much as you can into bitcoin, because it will probably do very, very well. Some altcoins will do even better.

Also think about what other opportunities you will lose with your wealth locked up in crypto.

Think about how you would feel if you needed to pay for something or buy something beyond your means, or if you had a family or medical emergency. Most people will not accept bitcoin as payment—and you wouldn't want to give it up, anyway.

Could that change?

Yes, of course. If we do get hyper-inflation, nobody will want your government's money. You'll need alternatives to cash. Balance is crucial in times of uncertainty.

Meanwhile, don't sweat the ups and downs. In this market, a 15-20% swing means nothing, it's just noise.

In the real world, people are struggling terribly and the global economy is on the brink of collapse. In the bitcoin world, everybody's hyped about the halving and $288,000 bitcoin and whatever else makes people think they'll get rich.

Don't worry about those 15-20% drops. It's crypto, that's something you'll see many, many times.

Worry about the things that really matter—your health, your friends, your family, and the things that are important to you.

Those things can disappear in an instant. Cryptocurrency will be around for a very, very long time.

Until next time, relax and enjoy the ride.

June 2020

[Note—I published this in the wake of race riots and anti-mask mania across the U.S.]

I'm starting to think 2020 is the year of awareness.

Awareness about race. Money. Politics. Power. Inequality. Identity. Public health.

And technology.

While not as visible or visceral as those larger issues, the world's collective response to COVID-19 created a new awareness about the value of digital technology. This awareness could have a profound impact on the spread of cryptocurrency.

Over the short term, it will not matter. Prices reflect the daily battles of bulls and bears.

Today's issue looks at the bigger context, a larger shift within the cryptosphere.

It's the shift from people like you and me to people like your boss and your parents.

Prepare for the early adopters

I report to baby boomers and I have friends who work for baby boomers. I know people in finance, as well as business owners and executives. Also, I work for the U.S. government, which is led by some of the world's *least* tech-driven leaders.

Everybody is using the internet for work this year. Not just email and Powerpoint, but videochats, online training, screen sharing, Slack, Zoom, cloud storage, you name it, they're doing it online, remotely, virtually.

Guess what's happening?

They're realizing with a little training and some small changes in habits, they can save a lot of time and money without losing too much productivity. Some even like it.

For many, banking from home is a life-saving convenience. Video conferences are cost-effective ways to connect with friends, family, and colleagues. Virtual paperwork really *is* easier than ink pad signature stamps. Downtown real estate really *is* too expensive. My millennial subordinates really *can be* productive without coming into the office.

You might not think these people matter for cryptocurrency. They embody the legacy system. They don't care about cryptographically-secure, time-stamped, distributed digital ledgers, nor do they think about the flaws of fiat money and inflationary central bank policies.

Yet, these people have money and power. They run our businesses and government. They hold as much as $70 trillion in assets, depending on what survey you believe.

And they are no longer skeptical about digital goods and services.

Inevitability is a selling point

This year, the demand for virtual services has exploded.

While some of this demand will subside as life goes back to normal, some will stick.

Some routine doctor visits and most consultations, many meetings, and almost every clerical or paperwork process will migrate to a digital platform. Companies will shift some positions to permanent telework. Mortgages and many routine financial transactions will settle using secure, internet-based commercial platforms. Companies will replace their payment processors with lower-cost, more nimble platforms like Stripe.

Even governments will change the way they deliver services and manage their money systems. Everybody wants to get rid of patchwork legacy systems, paper checks, physical banknotes, and layers of databases. China is testing its digital yuan. The U.S. Federal Reserve accelerated progress on its digital dollar.

None of these shifts *need to* include blockchain technology. Most won't. That's not the point.

The point is more and more people recognize the flaws in our commercial and financial systems.

COVID-19 has broken the status quo and governments have not offered any alternative. Meanwhile, DeFi has shown that you can manage financial systems without governments. Bitcoin has shown you can send money to people without banks. Altcoins have shown you can use money systems to solve social, political, and business problems.

True, on a small scale. This is a young technology, still developing.

But as a person in finance told me, lots of his clients have a sense that crypto "is the way everything's going." More people understand that crypto is not about creating a new Venmo, but rather, building global, permissionless networks that everybody can use.

Of course, it helps that rich people and investment funds started buying bitcoin as a way to gamble on their governments' recent money printing.

But those people are mostly not interested in building the financial networks of the future, they're just hoping bitcoin will boom and make them more money.

If that happens, they'll sell. If that doesn't happen, they'll sell. They'll only stick around long enough to find out which result they'll get.

We can take those people for granted. If anything, their money will push bitcoin into its next bull run (though I think we're already in the middle of one).

It's all those other people that will send bitcoin to those lofty, mythical prices everybody predicts, along with the mainstream adoption everybody wants. Normal people who believe this new technology will fix problems with the traditional financial system. Angry people looking for a way out, latching on to this new tech-nology. Old people staking a small claim to bitcoin as part of their legacy or retirement portfolio.

It will all seem more real because cryptocurrency has come so far since the 2017 boom. Many projects now have mainnets, dApps, and real usage beyond trading. Wall Street veterans now run crypto funds and crypto-related businesses. Universities teach blockchain. Some governments have crafted legal frameworks to protect and promote cryptocurrency.

Inevitability is a very compelling concept.

That's great, Mark. Wen moon?

Does that mean bitcoin will get a massive rush of money and innovation tomorrow?

No. It takes time for people to wrap their heads around what's going on. Awareness does not mean action.

Wall Street has only just started to corner the market for their clients. Bitcoin's Lightning Network hasn't caught on the way anybody expected and DeFi platforms still have operational, security, and regulatory issues to fix before most people (including myself) consider locking up their money in smart contracts and liquidity pools.

Your average person is worried about their job, their family, and so many other problems. Even if they had money to spare, they probably aren't going to put it into bitcoin. That's something *other* people do. It's too risky.

If you want that big, massive, life-changing bull market that sends prices into the stratosphere, *this is a good thing.*

You need people to commit to this market. They need to care so much that they're willing to suffer through 30-40% crashes, threats of government bans, failures with DeFi protocols, faulty oracles, high transaction fees, and the general complexity that has characterized cryptocurrency over the years.

Growth needs to come from conviction.

The good news is, conviction has entered the markets. If you're a premium subscriber, you have seen the data validating that statement. If you're not a premium subscriber, I don't want to digress too much, I hope you'll take it on faith that what I'm saying is true.

For the past few months, bitcoins have flowed into the hands of long-term HODLers and institutional investors—people who are willing to ride the market up and down. Based on past behavior, you're not going to get a lot of selling pressure from them until prices go very high, very quickly, and they start pulling their money out of the market.

Meanwhile, miner inventories continue to dwindle, as shown in the Bitcoin Miners Position Index and the cut in block rewards.

Sellers are leaving the market. Bitcoins are flowing to people with strong hands.

When will new buyers arrive?

I don't know, but Google Trends shows worldwide searches for bitcoin have gone up steadily since December 2019. In the past, that's signaled future growth.

What about altcoins?

This part of the market remains driven almost exclusively by individual investors and users, aka "retail." Only a handful of altcoins have enough liquidity for institutional investors looking to make an investment of any significant size on the open market.

They may buy alts in private deals, but you and I will never know about it.

Still, the alts have seen strength over the past year. Sentiment, activity, and interest in altcoins went up steadily for months.

While this hasn't shown up in price yet, it will soon. A lot of amateur investors are selling the pumps now, so it's hard to get a lot of momentum. That will change soon because the people buying either have conviction around these projects or enough savvy to ride the ups and downs without selling.

But bitcoin still leads. Altcoins make up barely one-quarter of the crypto market and almost no institutional investors can buy them, except for their personal use. You need to follow bitcoin. Where bitcoin goes, the market follows.

Where's bitcoin going?

Probably, up.

Private bitcoin funds have seen record-breaking growth this year. These funds only allow accredited investors, and they're raising money like crazy. Already, registered bitcoin funds hold 3% of the world's bitcoin. Who knows how much more is sitting in cold wallets and private accounts?

It's not just investors buying bitcoin. Traders are accumulating, too.

In May, derivatives platform Bakkt saw more physically-settled futures contracts than cash-settled contracts. It's one thing to trade paper derivatives for kicks. Once you take custody of bitcoin, you usually intend to use it.

All my contacts in finance are buying for themselves and their clients. These guys are not selling at $10k and shorting "all the way down." Yes, they hedge their bets with futures or options—but they do that so they *don't* have to sell their bitcoin. They're managing risks, not betting against themselves.

While Crypto Twitter and your Telegram group brag about shorting the top, the smart money is loading up on cheap bitcoin.

Meanwhile, you, me, and the OGs continue to use and accumulate. We don't worry about who sold the pump or got rekt. We're not timing the markets. We have strength and conviction.

Our strength and conviction will send bitcoin to the moon.

It may not happen overnight, but it won't take much new money to cause that boom everybody expects.

No place to go but up

Smart money knows something that's easy to forget when you're in the cryptosphere. What is that?

Crypto is tiny.

Sometimes, the numbers seem big. Binance is worth $2 billion. Coinbase, $8 billion. DeFi contracts hold over $1 billion in ETH. Brave browser has 13 million daily users. Bitcoin has almost $180 billion market cap.

Millions and billions. These seem like such big numbers.

In reality, those numbers are tiny.

Morgan Stanley makes $10 billion each quarter. BNY Mellon, Blackrock, State Street, Fidelity, and other medium-size Wall Street firms make somewhere between $12-18 billion each year.

Global investment portfolios include about *$40 trillion* in assets, possibly double that amount. The U.S. alone has more than $22 trillion in assets held by registered investment institutions, which does not include personal wealth and foreign accounts.

Plus, you can add some of the new money that countries just printed.

If you charted bitcoin on a pie graph of the world's wealth, you wouldn't even see it (I tried). I had to find another way to visualize it, with this image:

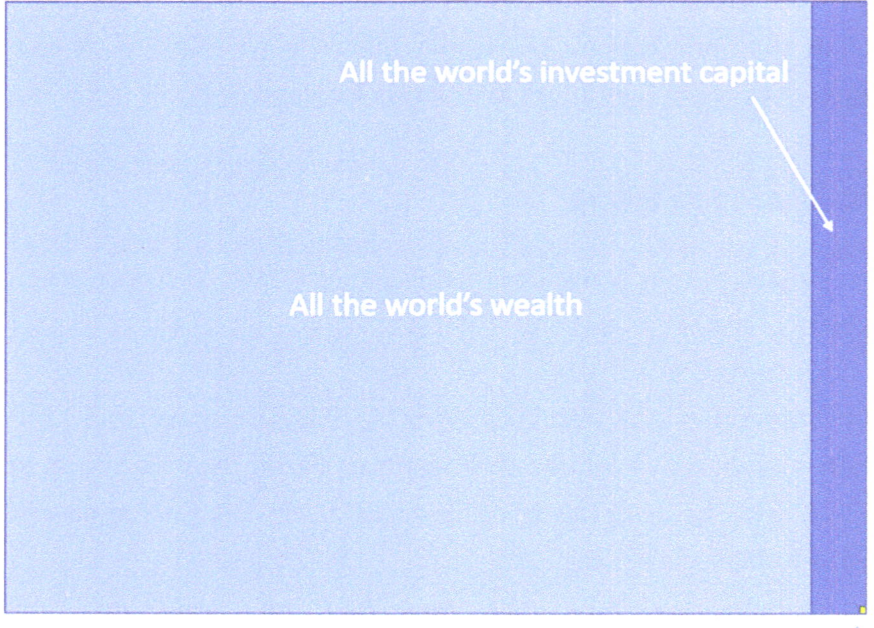

All the world's bitcoin

The rectangle represents the world's wealth ($1 quadrillion). The dark blue stripe represents the world's investment capital ($40 trillion), and the yellow pixel is bitcoin's slice of the pie. Tiny, even at $10,000.

And what about altcoins? Why don't I include the alts?

Because they don't register at all. Bitcoin takes up about 66% of the market, with another 10% in stablecoins. Altcoins make up the remainder—barely 24% total.

People drive markets

So why has bitcoin's price leveled off? Why are so many people still selling and shorting the market?

Because money doesn't drive markets. People do. As long as people want to cash out or play the market, it doesn't matter how much money's sitting on a bank ledger or in a safe deposit box.

Who's cashing out? Who's buying in?

That's what matters.

Does it seem odd that the so-called bitcoin maximalists and true believers keep selling/shorting at $10k (or so they claim), while financial professionals accumulate hundreds of thousands of bitcoins?

Isn't traditional finance supposed to crush bitcoin while maximalists carry the torch? Why are the pros buying while the "true believers" are selling?

It's all about mindset.

There is no reason to play day trader when we have such amazing things to look forward to.

I keep my eyes on the data from Glassnode, Delphi Digital, newsletters, and other research services. That's where you can learn about what people are doing to drive the markets. You can see where bitcoins are moving or what altcoins are getting inflows and usage. You can spot those big, huge shifts in the market and the behavior of people in the market.

Growth in bitcoin's Lightning Network, Ethereum 2.0, the latest mainnet launch or altcoin partnership—those things will matter, in time.

For now, it's all about people. Who's buying, who's selling, who's using.

Even if fundamentals mattered, how can anybody assess them now? All assets are topsy-turvy, from real estate to stocks to treasury notes. Valuations and metrics are falling apart. Correlations seem to have collapsed. Common sense seems to have disappeared.

Worldwide, investors hold $12 trillion of negative-yielding bonds and they're almost certainly going to buy more over the coming years.

The U.S. government flooded the market with dollars . . . *only to see the price of dollars go up*. In fact, USD has gone up 17% over the past two years and shows no signs of slowing down. What do you think will happen when oil markets recover and everybody suddenly needs petrodollars again?

Residential real estate prices in the U.S. keep rising even though 25% of workers have lost their jobs. The stock market's on course to recover all of its losses.

None of these things make sense.

Are we embarking on a new reality or are people just slow to catch up? I don't know.

If it's hard to make sense of traditional assets that have long price histories and well-established metrics, how can anybody expect to measure the "fundamental" value of cryptocurrency?

Stay diversified

For that reason, it's important to stay diversified.

I know it sounds terrible to say, especially when everybody's telling you this is the best time to buy bitcoin and I'm showing you all this bullish data and analysis.

For all we know, it could take years for bitcoin to get where we want it to go, even if its price goes up. Meanwhile, you will need fiat to pay bills and buy things.

Also, if you keep all your wealth in bitcoin, you will miss chances to invest in other, possibly better opportunities.

Any private companies that are raising money now and have strong balance sheets, teams you can believe in, and good products or services—those companies will dominate the next decade. You can get a 1,000x return from owning a small stake in one of those companies, with no volatility and (in the U.S.) tax advantages to boot.

Also look for traditional investments, maybe even business ventures.

The world is changing quickly and drastically. You don't want your whole financial fate tied to bitcoin. If we get the 10-100x returns everybody predicts, you won't need to put much money in now. You can look forward to a life-changing, once-in-a-generation windfall. A 2% investment could double your net worth. How greedy do you need to be?

Just because Stock-to-Flow says bitcoin will go to $288,000, you can't ever know how long that will take or what might happen along the way. The model could fail.

Never put all your eggs in one basket.

Over the next few years, I expect to see crypto move from a tiny, niche commodity to an established, robust asset class. Today, people are suffering from economic uncertainty, personal hardship, and pandemic disease. Massive social and political movements are sweeping the world. Crypto isn't really on people's minds.

We have the good fortune to own a small stake in the financial networks of the future. Let's hope others will join us, in time.

I suspect they will. Meanwhile, relax and enjoy the ride.

July 2020

When I worked in politics, it was my first exposure to wealth. As the son of a public attorney and an ESOL teacher, I had no concept of money—let alone a world where money seemed endless.

A lobbyist could pay $3,000 to eat breakfast with a member of Congress, and it was considered an incidental expense on the monthly financial report. Candidates could raise hundreds of millions of dollars for campaigns that were almost destined to fail, and it was considered normal.

At H&R Block, we paid a lobbyist $20,000 each month to play an occasional round of golf with members and their staffs . . . and the SVP asked my boss to spend *more* money because we weren't getting enough results.

Often, I'd read bills with line items that spanned the width of a page. Budget tables would include four- or five-digit numbers, with a header "in billions of dollars."

Yes, *billions*. Numbers so big, nobody could fit them on a piece of paper.

Take a look at this budget report:

Table 3.

CBO's Estimate of the Effects of the President's Budget Proposals

Billions of Dollars

| | | | | | | | | | | | | Total | |
| | | | | | | | | | | | | 2018–2022 | 2018–2027 |
	2017	2018	2019	2020	2021	2022	2023	2024	2025	2026	2027	2018–2022	2018–2027
Deficit in CBO's June 2017 Baseline	-693	-563	-689	-775	-879	-1,027	-1,057	-1,083	-1,225	-1,352	-1,463	-3,933	-10,112
Effects of the President's Proposals[a]													
Outlays													
Mandatory													
Reduce federal spending for health care	0	-31	-25	-98	-153	-187	-222	-243	-282	-304	-347	-493	-1,891
Reduce federal spending for income security	0	-3	-11	-19	-23	-26	-29	-29	-26	-34	-38	-83	-238
Provide mandatory funding for infrastructure	0	5	25	40	50	40	20	10	5	5	0	160	200
Reduce subsidies for student loans	0	-2	-4	-6	-8	-9	-11	-13	-14	-16	-17	-29	-100
Other proposals	0	-6	-5	-15	4	7	9	11	17	-10	-16	-15	-3
Subtotal, mandatory	0	-37	-21	-99	-129	-175	-233	-264	-300	-358	-417	-460	-2,033
Discretionary													
Reduce spending for overseas contingency operations	0	-7	-26	-46	-67	-86	-96	-101	-105	-108	-110	-231	-752
Other defense	0	30	45	49	50	49	48	47	45	43	42	224	448
Other nondefense	0	-10	-53	-88	-127	-152	-177	-199	-223	-247	-271	-430	-1,548
Subtotal, discretionary	0	14	-34	-85	-144	-189	-225	-254	-283	-311	-340	-438	-1,851
Net interest	0	*	1	*	-5	-12	-22	-35	-51	-69	-91	-16	-285
Total Effect on Outlays	0	-23	-54	-184	-278	-376	-480	-553	-635	-739	-849	-914	-4,170
Revenues													
Repeal and replace the Affordable Care Act	0	-55	-60	-85	-100	-105	-115	-120	-120	-120	-120	-405	-1,000
Increase federal employees' retirement contributions	0	2	4	7	9	11	13	14	15	15	15	33	103
Other proposals	0	*	2	5	1	1	*	-1	-1	-1	-1	8	3
Total Effect on Revenues	0	-53	-54	-74	-91	-93	-103	-107	-106	-106	-107	-365	-894
Total Effect on the Deficit[b]	0	-30	*	110	187	282	377	447	528	633	742	549	3,276
Deficit Under the President's Budget as Estimated by CBO	-693	-593	-689	-664	-692	-745	-681	-636	-696	-719	-720	-3,383	-6,836
Memorandum:													
Total Effect on Noninterest Outlays	0	-23	-55	-184	-273	-364	-458	-518	-584	-670	-757	-898	-3,885

Sources: Congressional Budget Office, staff of the Joint Committee on Taxation.

That top left number isn't -$693. It's -$693,000,000,000.

Our "big" is not so big

Sometimes we look at crypto and see big numbers. For example, $170 billion in bitcoin, $12 billion in stablecoins, $3.5 billion market cap for Cardano, $3 billion in Graystone Bitcoin Trust, $1.5 billion assets on DeFi lending platforms, 75 million bitcoin wallets, 15 million active daily users of Brave browser, and so on.

Those numbers are big—but the world is so much bigger.

On top of hundreds of trillions of dollars locked up in real assets like property, cars, land, buildings, clothes, and collectibles, the world has at least $100 trillion in government debt, $200 trillion in corporate and household debt, and $400 trillion in financial products like derivatives and collateralized loan obligations.

Those numbers exceed $1 quadrillion.

ONE. QUADRILLION.

All of that wealth can get recorded on a blockchain and exchanged using cryptocurrency. Every single penny.

So many ways to capture wealth

Think about all the ways cryptocurrency will capture this wealth.

For example, I just reported to premium subscribers about a decentralized exchange about to revamp its platform.

As part of the revamp, the team will create decentralized margin accounts for traders and stakers, plus liquidity pools for exchange assets and derivatives. In one sentence, a half-dozen ways to capture wealth—with almost all of the benefits going to token holders.

Two more ways to capture wealth?

Token sets and PIES, which offer non-custodial access to diversified investment portfolios.

And what about non-financial markets?

Look at energy. The world wastes a lot of energy. Some places produce more than they need while other places face chronic shortages. That's a hard problem to solve with traditional technology, but cryptocurrency offers a potentially easier solution.

Once you tokenize energy consumption as a cryptocurrency, you can more easily create secondary markets and efficient distribution channels. You can embed carbon emissions credits, rebates, and incentives into the tokens. Power plants and distributors can mint their own tokens when they create energy and burn those tokens as people consume it.

More ways to capture wealth.

What about DAOs for corporate and community assets? Security tokens for real estate development?

With cryptocurrency, the possibilities are infinite. It's just a matter of building the right platforms.

Fortunately, we have a lot of people building those platforms. They toil in the shadow of bitcoin and DeFi, but their work will get its proper recognition in time. They've barely scratched the surface of what they can do.

Slowly, then all at once

As bitcoin's price continues moving sideways and DeFi tokens seem like the only altcoins going up, you may feel like crypto is stagnant. Or, if you missed the DeFi pumps, you may feel like you're too late.

That's how it goes. Take DeFi, for example. Until June, you probably didn't think much of it. Now, it's all everybody talks about.

Some of these DeFi projects spent three or more years in development. When I started working on *Consensusland*, I consulted with a few projects, including Aave. At that time, they called themselves ETHLend and had barely finished setting up their team.

Who would have known they'd emerge as a top DeFi project two years later?

It takes a long time to become an overnight sensation.

While it's hard to wait, it's important. Everybody wants the moonshot NOW, not next year or the year after.

But we need momentum and a strong narrative. The vast majority of people do not understand what's going on in this space. Frankly, a lot of people in this space don't know what's going on, they just want fast money.

But fast money is hard money—hard to find, hard to get, hard to keep. Slow money is easy money—you put in all the effort upfront, then let time and markets do the work for you.

For me, this boredom is progress. It means people are committed to results, not money. They're pouring time, effort, and labor into building new products and services.

That's real passion and conviction, not dreams of Lambos.

We only benefit if these projects succeed, and they will only succeed if they have enough time and space to do so.

Rest assured, Lambos will come. As technology sticks and networks grow, prices will follow.

We'll get Lambos when the time's right.

Thank you central banks

But passion doesn't move markets. Money does.

With a global recession and pandemic disease, with so many sectors of the world's economies struggling or non-functional . . . where does that market-moving money come from?

The banks, of course.

In the U.S., money in bank deposits and money market accounts, generally considered household wealth or "M2" by economists, rose $3 trillion from March to June to its all-time high. That money is collecting almost zero interest (and for some accounts, costing monthly maintenance fees).

Over the same time period, the stock market fell slightly—a big drop in March followed by recovery. Obviously, relatively little of that new money went into equities.

Some, yes, but people can only buy so many junk bonds and businesses with no profits before they realize there's not enough economic activity to give them a decent return on their investments.

Besides, millions of people have no jobs and most don't know when they'll go back to work.

As a result, we have trillions of dollars sitting on the sidelines, locked away in bank vaults. From January to May, the average U.S. household savings rate went from 8% to 33%. That's insane, by far the highest rate on record.

Many other developed countries see the same phenomenon.

More money, more problems

Many people think all that new money will cause inflation. BRRRR, they say.

Maybe, maybe not.

I've seen people point to rising food prices as evidence of inflation, but even before massive government stimulus, we had a global wheat shortage and trade barriers pushing up prices going back to 2019, long before BRRRR. COVID-19 brought supply chain disruptions and mass-destruction of food inputs. Maybe higher prices reflect market conditions, not BRRRR money printing?

(Neither of us have enough evidence to know.)

Also, despite Twitter's insistence, lots of U.S. investors did not spend their stimulus checks on cryptocurrency. Worldwide, hardly any new money went into crypto—the total market cap has gone up only about $100 billion since BRRRR started.

Why is that?

Because money can't cause inflation if it's not circulating around the economy. And right now, it's not circulating.

Instead of lending out money, banks have cut off loans for commercial real estate, residential investment properties, and small businesses. They expect the economy will get worse. They won't take on the risks.

In response, the Fed is basically paying banks to lend, setting up facilities to swap their debt for cash, offering banks up to 7% premiums (pure profits), and back-stopping up to 95% of the loan amounts.

And *still* the banks can't find enough people to lend money to.

Bailouts, handouts, and quantitative easing have pumped trillions of dollars in new money into the world's financial system, but that money has nowhere to go.

Yield, where are ye?

Thanks to the pandemic, you can't invest in the real economy anymore. Nobody's making movies. Nobody's going on cruises. Nobody's playing sports. Nobody knows when (or if) building starts and big infrastructure projects will get off the ground.

Thanks to central banks, you can't invest in debt markets or equities, either. Bonds yield almost nothing (sometimes, less than nothing). Cash and cash equivalents offer even worse returns.

Stock markets are full of businesses that have no profits or customers. Many corporations stopped buying back shares. High P/E ratios suggest poor future returns and nobody knows whether the economy will rebound. Profits have dried up, making it hard for companies to pay dividends.

People like to say bitcoin doesn't offer dividends, but what happens when your stocks don't either?

Bonds don't offer a decent shot at making money, either.

Most major economies offer negative-yielding debt and U.S. treasury rates remain effectively zero. Corporate debt is almost worthless, outside of a few bankrupt businesses waiting for vulture capitalists to take them over.

Private equity, perhaps? Perhaps not. Start-ups are strapped for cash and struggling to conquer COVID-19.

You can't even invest in banks anymore. European banks are barely solvent and the U.S. Federal Reserve barred banks from buying back stock and raising dividends, two of the biggest incentives for investors.

China and U.S. trade relations have fallen apart, so you can't invest in China. The E.U. might fall apart, so you can't invest in Europe.

A new investing paradigm

As an investor, you want to find ways to maximize opportunities and minimize risks. In this new investment landscape, that means making unusual choices.

For example, money has started flowing to emerging markets, despite an ever-growing list of countries defaulting or restructuring their debt. Why do investors feel compelled to buy investments in countries that probably will never repay them?

As always, you have speculators looking to flip bonds, but mostly, it's just investors looking for yields. Unlike junk bonds and penny stocks, emerging markets have special financial instruments that protect investors from some of the downside risks.

Plus, these countries have many ways to raise cash, unlike corporations, which have few.

Meanwhile, massive QE suggests the value of the dollar will fall, making emerging market debts easier to repay over time.

Why buy junk bonds and penny stocks when you can get a higher return with less risk in emerging market debt?

Return of the liquidity trap

This problem exists because of the so-called liquidity trap— lots of money, little yield, and people too scared to spend.

When you have no incentive to invest, you don't invest. Why give up cash and property when your expected risk-adjusted returns are basically zero?

Some people think that this liquidity trap has created a massive "everything" bubble, where equities, businesses, bonds, property, and everything else gets pumped up beyond their "real" values.

Surely *something* has to give, right?

Economist Robert Shiller won a Nobel prize for his work on assets and how assets acquire value. He discovered that there is no intrinsic value to anything. Production and consumption costs, dividends and P/E ratios, and other metrics do not reflect the actual price of an asset at any given time.

Price is a function of people's actions and behaviors. Markets are not rational. Asset bubbles only pop when people stop believing in them. Until then, they generally go up, sometimes forever.

Shiller would say "it's more nuanced than that," which is true, but I don't publish *Crypto is Nuanced*, I publish *Crypto is Easy*. I'm summarizing decades of research into two paragraphs. That's the easiest way I can explain it.

In other words, the bubble may never pop—if it's even a bubble in the first place. It will just persist, skewing people's economic decisions, until people decide to change their behaviors.

Money now, crypto later

Those behaviors will have to change eventually.

Money tends to flow into the hands of whoever can do the most with it. As asset prices rise, investments no longer produce as much yield as they did before. You need to spend more to make less.

Humans will adapt. Money always finds another opportunity.

With $16 trillion sitting in bank accounts, $22 trillion in U.S.-registered investment funds, and at least $40 trillion in private wealth held offshore, plus trillions more in cash and real estate, there's plenty of money searching for opportunities.

Recently, banks and large investment institutions got U.S. regulators to change the rules keeping them from investing in private equity, one of the riskiest markets on earth. You can expect the search for yield will push their boundaries even further.

At what point do money managers decide their fiduciary duties compel them to put some money into the best performing asset of the past ten years? To place a small wager on a small altcoin project?

When do financial advisors tell their clients to put a little money into a bitcoin fund, "just in case" it goes up?

How low do bond yields and stock dividends go before casual investors rebalance into bitcoin, "the fastest horse" as investment legend Paul Tudor Jones calls it? When do banks start taking crypto deposits?

They just need to see prices go up long enough to trust the market will continue moving up. Once we get past that psychological hurdle, everything will change.

With cryptocurrency, people will escape the liquidity trap.

Big tailwinds

As you may have read in *Bitcoin or Bust: Wall Street's Entry Into Cryptocurrency*, I expect traditional financial institutions to start talking about crypto to their clients.

If that seems odd, remember how JP Morgan blasted crypto as a scam, then created its own crypto and, later, brought on Coinbase and Gemini as customers.

These conversations will start as discussions about portfolio diversification and inflation hedges.

Advisors and money managers will note "it's the way everything's going" or remark about a weakening dollar as a reason to have a small allocation of crypto (or at least, bitcoin).

Or, some rich people will hear about crypto from their kids or friends and ask their financial advisors to "throw a few shekels" at it.

Your parents' friends will mention putting a little money into a bitcoin fund "just in case it goes up." People in suits will cite research that a little crypto boosts returns while reducing volatility (which is true).

Crypto funds and exchanges will take out ads shilling their products and platforms. Fidelity will offer bitcoin. Coinbase will go public.

At the same time, several emerging trends will bolster their message:

1. People starting to get so fed up with governments they're choosing to opt-out of "the system," with cryptocurrency as a peaceful, easy way to do so.
2. Old people and business leaders finally realizing the value and inevitability of digital technology. Some will join the early adopters as the technology grows, making it seem safer for everybody else.
3. Developers creating useful products that use cryptocurrency. DeFi is just the start—and these products go way beyond the tentative experiments of IBM, Microsoft, Ernst & Young, MoneyGram, JP Morgan, and everybody doing business with VeChain.
4. Prices starting to rise. We're on the cusp of a new bull market.
5. Generation Z making money. At least, if the economy turns around. Already, 30% of them say they plan to buy

crypto—enough to double the total number of crypto users and send DOGE to the moon.

These trends will take time to play out, but they will result in something far bigger than a 10x pump in LEND's price.

What does that mean for us?

That means we don't need to stress about today's prices.

We don't need to try to play the markets, trade in and out, or worry we've missed out on any coin that has already gone up 400% in two weeks.

We're so early, we have the luxury of time. When you depend on other people to make your crypto valuable, you have to give them time to do so. Markets move fast. People do not.

This is a time-tested, can't-miss approach to building wealth.

Robert Kiyosaki calls it seeing with your mind. Others have called it skating to the puck.

Most people focus only on what's in front of them. We focus on what's beyond, stake our claims, and wait for everybody else to follow.

Because of our good timing and dumb luck, we have a chance to catch all the dips, get free crypto, and buy stakes in the financial networks of the future with fairly little risk.

Meanwhile, we have more than enough upside to make up for any "bad" choices we make now.

The mainstream does not see this yet. They're seeing with their eyes, not their minds.

Don't stress the dips, don't worry about the crashes, and don't dismiss new projects simply because they seem amateur, esoteric, or their price hasn't gone up yet.

The world is struggling with pandemic disease and financial crises. Savings rates are going up in every country, even countries experiencing true inflation like Turkey and Lebanon.

Yields on traditional investments have plummeted while yields on crypto have boomed.

Traditional financial systems are increasingly unable to serve the needs of too many people. Politicians don't seem to be doing anything about it.

Yet, there is more money in the world economy than ever before.

Where will the money go?

If you're reading this, you already know the answer.

Relax and enjoy the ride.

August 2020

Cryptocurrency is full of people who believe in old economic theories that have never been tried in the real world. There's an almost zealous adherence to esoteric principles that seem to have no place in modern psychology, behavioral economics, and politics.

Fitting, perhaps, for a niche technology whose earliest followers—and most ardent advocates—came to it as an escape from convention. You would expect them to hold unconventional beliefs.

For me, bitcoin is not about economic liberation or freedom from corrupt authorities. It's about the potential for a new world order based on open, permissionless financial networks and trustless, censorship-resistant communities. Monetary innovation and choice. Inclusive markets.

If we can get to that point, we'll have economic liberation and freedom from corrupt authorities. We won't need theories to get us there.

People are losing faith in their leaders and questioning the traditional financial system. Investors have no good places to put their money anymore. Rich people want to protect their wealth against currency devaluation and reckless governments. Businesses need better digital goods and services to prosper in the post-COVID-19 world. Everybody worries about how long our economic crisis will last, and what will happen to them before it ends.

These are real problems, today.

Now is not the time to obsess about the supposed Cantillon effect of central banks or the cruel misery of fiat.

We're at the start of a massive shift in global monetary thought—except this time, it will not come from economists or political theorists, but from entrepreneurs, developers, mathematicians, and common men and women like you and me.

For the first time, we can test economic concepts in the real world. In doing so, we can create better markets, fairer economies, and stronger commercial networks.

Just as telescopes forced us to rethink our assumptions about the world and electricity forced us to rethink our assumptions about physics, cryptocurrency will force us to rethink our assumptions about money.

What discoveries will we find? What innovations will we create?

We will find out.

Eventually.

After all, people need to make money first.

"Price go up"

I expect a massive, long, powerful cryptocurrency bull market. This bull market will be driven by two things:

1. Decentralized financial platforms that make it easy for smart money and insiders to get unlimited access to cheap, easy cash.

2. Centralized financial platforms that make it easy for anybody to buy cryptocurrency.

But bitcoin will not succeed on greed alone. Altcoins will not thrive from pure speculation.

Ten trillion dollars will not flow into crypto on wings and prayers, no matter how bad the world's economy gets, how scared its rich people get, or how mad its poor people get.

At some point, you need conviction and a reality check.

Do people really care about their investment or do they just want to make money? Does this technology really have legs to stand on or is it a shot in the dark?

At this moment, it's clear: conviction has entered the markets and the technology is real.

Thanks to incredible innovations among cryptocurrency developers and blockchain engineers, we now have actual products and services running on cryptocurrency. DeFi may dominate the headlines today, but FOMO can't hide advances in tokenomics, scaling, decentralized governance, and blockchain technology's integration with real-world processes.

Not to mention the infrastructure around buying, selling, and using cryptocurrency is easier, safer, and better-regulated than ever before.

Walmart, Visa, IBM, Citigroup, and UPS are adopting blockchain technology to track their supply chains and facilitate cross-border transactions.

Fidelity, JPMorgan, and CashApp offer crypto products and services to their clients. PayPal and Facebook will soon join them.

Some cryptocurrency projects are working with governments on forensics, blockchain-based public services, and commercial innovation.

Bitmain, Coinbase, Ripple, and Ant Group have all said they plan to go public. U.S. regulators said banks can store cryptocurrency for their clients.

Over $100 billion dollars came into the cryptocurrency market this summer alone.

Looking at on-chain metrics—insights into the sentiment and behavior of people holding and using bitcoin—you see the same patterns and trends that we saw at the beginning of every previous bull run.

Altcoin projects have persisted through two or more years of funding carnage. Investors have held steady through 85% drops (99% drops for some projects).

Nobody is going to give up now.

COVID-19 Comes First

Medical science has tackled COVID-19 with incredible fervor and speed. Finally, we're seeing the results.

The world has ramped up the production of medical supplies, tests, and personal protective equipment while accelerating vaccine development and disease tracking.

We have several promising vaccine candidates and, at least in the U.S., enough capacity to quickly get hundreds of millions of doses into the hands of medical professionals within weeks of confirming whether any of these vaccines work.

We've discovered a drug, Remdesivir, that reduces COVID-19 symptoms and shortens the length of hospital stays for people who are severely infirmed. In other words, with this drug, people get less sick, need less care, and die less often.

Once we confirm the proper dosage and administration, we can make it a standard of care and possibly (eventually) allow doctors to treat COVID-19 on an outpatient basis. You would call your doctor, tell him/her your symptoms, and if it sounds like COVID-19, get a script for some drugs and quarantine for two weeks. That would be amazing (but let's not get ahead of ourselves).

We're pretty sure monoclonal antibodies work, too. With this technology, you can take a pill that gives your body COVID-19 antibodies. These antibodies wear off quickly but they provide the same protection you'd get with a vaccine, albeit temporarily. If effective, this treatment could serve as a key line of defense while scientists and drug companies ramp up vaccine production and distribution.

We also have preliminary data showing humidifiers cut down on the spread of COVID-19. This will matter more during the winter, but you can't ignore the significance: simply humidifying buildings and households will keep COVID-19 from spreading.

Of course, if everybody wore masks all the time, we would pretty much be able to go back to normal. Yes, people would still get sick, but it wouldn't be a public health emergency.

Unfortunately, that's not realistic. Too many people refuse to do that.

Why do I bring this up? What does this have to do with bitcoin?

I want to give you hope that within the next year or less, we will put COVID-19 behind us.

At that point, we can get back to normal economic activity. People will get their jobs back or find new ones. Businesses will recover. Confidence will return to households.

This is essential for cryptocurrency's success.

Nobody buys bitcoin when they're scared. They use their money for rent, food, and "things."

When you're about to get evicted or worried about losing your job or business, you don't usually speculate on innovative financial technology, no matter what the upside is.

You might hoard, worry, starve, protest, fight, revolt, or submit to tyrants, but you're not going to buy bitcoin.

What comes next?

Once we tame COVID-19 and life starts to get back to normal—whatever "normal" means in the post-COVID-19 world—humanity will have massive problems to deal with.

People will realize just how much minorities and poor people suffered under COVID-19 while white people and white-collar workers largely did ok. Governments will have massive budget deficits. Central banks will have bloated balance sheets. Some countries will default on their debt or replace their currencies. The global economy may take a very long time to recover.

And yet, no matter how gloomy the future seems, humanity always wins.

We have an amazing capacity to learn, change, and persist. We embrace new concepts when they solve our problems or make our lives better. We reject old concepts when experience shows us a better way.

To succeed, all cryptocurrency needs to do is one thing: give humans a better way.

That is the next challenge for cryptocurrency.

The money will come. You can take that for granted.

The question is what will we do with that money? Will we just recycle it from one stablecoin to another to generate yield? Will we use it to pump up the price of Bitcoin so we can sell it to somebody dumber or more greedy than us?

Sadly, yes.

But we will also pave the roads for the financial engines of the future.

As decentralized financial platforms mature and more people grow weary of incompetent governments and closed financial systems, they will create their own non-governmental organizations. They will organize themselves according to their principles and their interests, with rules embedded in their currencies and a blockchain to guarantee everybody will get the result they expect.

When people build businesses on these networks or start their own, they're not going to hire a crew of blockchain developers to design their token and all the infrastructure necessary to support it.

They'll use Aragon or DAOstack to program a token that provides the right incentives to support their project, with smart contracts that fit their needs. Then, they'll go about their business.

Like we use a word processor for today's publications, people will use a DAO for tomorrow's business structures. In one step, they will have a tool for raising funds, organizing workers, rewarding contributors, borrowing money, and managing workflows.

This will be as revolutionary as corporations when first developed in Renaissance Italy.

When you stand up a business that spans all seven continents and need to work with people you've never known, never met, and over whom you have no control or authority, you will look into a launching DAO much the same as today you look at incorporating.

"There's an app for that" will morph into "there's a token for that."

This is the world we are moving towards. New forms of governance and finance that seem bizarre and complicated. Ideas that stretch the boundaries of conventional thought. Products that test the limits of regulations and technology.

For example, yEarn Finance, a platform for finding the best lending rates on stablecoins. This project places governance entirely in the hands of token holders. It has no foundation, investors, or management. It's just a computer program. Nothing else.

Its token, YFI, is now worth $6,000.

Vive la révolution

As more projects like YFI gain momentum and prices go up, you will hear people revert to the old, trite arguments over what is money and what is not money.

They will focus on cryptocurrency as a transactional medium or investment, rather than a way for humans to operate in trustless environments.

They'll miss the true revolution—humans organizing themselves without a central authority to coerce them into doing things against their own best judgment. Breaking down the intermediaries and gatekeepers that cause bottlenecks, complexities, costs, and conflict. Promoting choice and community without undermining consensus and governance. Creating fairer, more inclusive financial and social networks.

The great benefit of having programmable money is not that it's better than what we have now, but that it gives you the ability to choose between the systems you want to use—and the opportunity to create your own, at global scale.

All from your laptop.

But not yet

Over the next few years, people will mostly not think about that. Everybody will focus on price.

I will, too.

In fact, a good deal of my premium content focuses on price, markets, and the opportunity to make money—or at least, better decisions about what we do with our money.

If people were naturally kind and generous, we would not need money, nor need to worry about how to get more of it.

But people are not naturally kind and generous. Therefore, when a once-in-a-generation opportunity presents itself, we need to take advantage of the opportunity.

That's ok.

In five years, you will not have a chance to get 20-30x returns from cryptocurrency, let alone the so-called moonshots you're dreaming about.

If history serves as our guide, you can expect the crypto market will get too big, many projects will fail, and governments will regulate the gains into the hands of rich people and insiders.

Cryptocurrency will still serve a valuable role and do all the things I said above, but you and I will no longer have a chance to make money off of that. As always, those opportunities will go to the wealthy and well-connected. We'll just use the platforms they create.

Today, we have a short window of opportunity to stake our claims to the financial networks of the future. We can't let this opportunity pass us by.

Bitcoin is about to start a huge bull run. During that run, it will crash. Not a 10% drop now and then, but six or seven gut-wrenching, 30-40% crashes that will shake your faith in its future.

Altcoins should follow bitcoin's path upward. Some will do even better, possibly much better.

Just keep in mind: if you *only* care about making money, you're missing the whole point.

If you get wrapped up in Cantillon effects and Austrian economics, take a step back. Look beyond theory and ideology. See beyond the investment opportunity. Think out of both sides of your head.

Cryptocurrency does not just fill an economic or financial need.

It fills a human need.

A token for every person and every purpose.

That's the revolution.

Relax and enjoy the ride.

September 2020

From 1957 to 1958, the United States suffered a recession on the heels of a pandemic flu outbreak. Unemployment hit its highest level in decades. Prices rose as the economy shrank, whacking workers with the double whammy—less money, higher prices.

In response, the government cut interest rates, lengthened unemployment benefits, and accelerated government construction projects. Within a year, the U.S. economy recovered.

In hindsight, few economists blame the flu for the recession, though at least 100,000 people died in the U.S. (one million people worldwide). Data suggest the natural end of a business cycle caused the recession, exacerbated by a series of rate hikes by the Federal Reserve.

Scientists produced a flu vaccine, people adjusted, and the economy recovered.

While COVID-19 is far more deadly, contagious, and difficult to treat than the 1957 flu (it's not even a type of flu), it likewise received an aggressive public response, as did the recession it left in its wake. Also, like the 1957-58 recession, historians will realize disease did not cause this most recent financial downturn, it simply led the way.

As I said in last month's issue, I expect we will put COVID-19 behind us by next summer. Medical science is too swift. Its discoveries are too compelling.

By the end of the year, we will probably know everything we need to know to crush "the global bastard" and get back to normal—whatever "normal" means in the post-COVID-19 world. It may take many months longer to get vaccines and treatments to everybody who needs them, but it will happen.

Perhaps we will fall into another Great Depression before we get there.

Hopefully not.

Humans are incredibly resilient. Economies adjust. Leaders and entrepreneurs find a better way.

The financial crisis of 2020 saw massive, coordinated government financial interventions on a level and sophistication never attempted before. While it's too soon to think our economies will recover soon, it's not too soon to think about what will happen once they do.

At that point, we will have to confront all the problems we had before pandemic disease and economic crisis consumed the world's attention.

The list of problems is long, far longer than I have room to include in this issue. It includes racism, inequality, poverty, reckless government monetary policies, and an almost unbreakable commitment to debt, deficits, and spending among the world's leading economies.

Meanwhile, we continue to endure the slow whittling down of public discourse, the gradual destruction of free markets, and the silent erosion of the value of labor, as measured in money.

Cryptocurrency can fix all of that.

And what does the cryptosphere care about?

Sushi, hot dogs, pickles, and pasta. "Price go up." Moon.

Awesome tech, LOVE the mission, freedom and all that . . . should I buy that latest DeFi token?

A revolution, if you can keep it

Cryptocurrency will fundamentally change our modern notion of money, wealth, privacy, property, and commerce.

For the first time, we can create financial networks that *everybody* can participate in.

You don't need to know somebody who knows somebody who can get you in, nor do you need to meet somebody else's standard for what "qualifies" you for admission. You just need to download the app or visit the website.

Everybody can participate in finance, join a group, start a business, and trade property no matter where they live. how much money they have, what political or religious organization they belong to, their family's status, their race or religion, their level of education, or their nationality.

Computer programs can't discriminate. Algorithms can't shut you out.

No lobbyist can change bitcoin's rules. No autocrat can punish it to silence.

The three Ds of the next bull run—DeFi, DAOs, and DEXs—will test the limits of monetary thought and yield paradigm-shifting discoveries for the benefit of all humanity, not just the rich and powerful.

These discoveries will be every bit as profound as penicillin, steam power, and electricity.

For the first time, we can test monetary concepts in the real world. We can go beyond the efficient market theory and Pareto charts. We can observe monetary policy in its purest form, without political influence and interference.

What discoveries will we find? What innovations will we create?

Everything is possible.

But money comes first

Possibilities abound—and we'll get around to that.

First, the money. After all, it's not called crypto*makethe-worldbetter*. It's called crypto*currency*. Literally, the technology of money.

No matter how much good it does for humanity, somebody will get rich from it.

In some ways, that's the whole point. Create value and ye shall receive value. What good is a new money system if nobody uses it?

Consider Ampleforth, a financial network that rebalances users' funds whenever the value of its token, AMPL, moves too much. Theoretically, users can preserve the purchasing power of their money as the network grows or shrinks. The number of AMPL tokens will go up or down based on an algorithm designed to keep the token price stable.

Will it work in the real world?

We shall see. Meanwhile, you can play the rebalance for SICK gains, bro, as long as you don't get rekt.

Some cryptocurrency teams like GoodDollar have started exploring universal basic income. They're trying to figure out how to give everybody access to money without moral hazards and market inefficiencies.

Will it work in the real world?

We shall see. Did you get my link for the airdrop? Easy money!

Rightfully So

These experiments and dozens of others will lead to profound insights into humans, markets, and finance.

They will lay the building blocks for the financial networks of the future. Just as telescopes forced us to rethink our assumptions about the earth and electricity forced us to rethink our assumptions about physics, cryptocurrency will force us to rethink our assumptions about money.

This will take time to sink in. Technology moves fast. People do not.

Perhaps we can be forgiven for obsessing about staking rewards and yield farming. After all, in a few years, rewards will slow down and yields will fall—*by design*.

Now, it's never been so easy to buy into the same types of wealth creation machines that wealthy people have used for so long to make money off of their money. We owe it to ourselves to participate.

In doing so, we play a small role in weaving the financial tapestry of the 21st Century. We risk our fortunes in support of this new asset class and the technology behind it.

It's only fair we benefit from that.

Wealth is not the goal—it's the outcome

As cryptocurrency markets grow and prices go up, you will hear people revert to the old, trite arguments over what is money and what is not money.

They will focus on cryptocurrency as a way to transact or invest, rather than a way to create trustless networks for the benefit of all. Even bitcoin maximalists will fall into this trap.

They'll miss the true revolution—humans organizing themselves without a central authority to coerce them into doing things against their own best judgment. People breaking down the intermediaries and gatekeepers that cause bottlenecks, complexities, costs, and conflicts.

They won't realize cryptocurrency gives humanity a chance to promote choice and create communities without undermining consensus and governance. Nor will they care how cryptocurrency can create fairer, more inclusive financial and social networks.

That's ok. We will.

While the rest of the world will obsess over central bank actions, the intrinsic value of money, and archaic financial concepts, we will pave the financial roads of the future. We don't need to wait for economists and political theorists to present solutions. Once we have an idea, we can put it into action. Nobody can stop us from doing so.

As a result, the financial discoveries of the future will not come from academics and politicians. They'll come from entrepreneurs, computer scientists, developers, mathematicians, and common people like you and me.

And we will reap the benefits.

Will we use our good fortune to build open, permissionless financial networks and trustless, censorship-resistant communities? Promote monetary innovation, privacy, and inclusive markets? Make money systems that allow the poor and marginalized to contribute to the world's markets and, as a result, build their own wealth and financial security?

Or will we recycle made-up tokens from one lending platform to another? Pump up DeFi schemes? Use cheap cash to drive up prices so we can sell our stakes to somebody dumber or more greedy than we are?

The urgency of now

In the midst of worldwide economic decline, political discord, pandemic disease, and social crisis, we are fortunate. We have the time, money, and opportunity to invest in the financial networks of the future.

While we will benefit from doing this, we have an obligation to go further.

We can take the gains for granted. This means we don't have to stress about the ups and downs, mess with latest meme token, or FOMO into the next DeFi pump coin. Opportunities abound. Altcoin projects are doing amazing things. Bitcoin's Lightning Network has grown strong enough to support new payment rails and settlement platforms for all sorts of financial transactions.

As a result, we can focus on things that carry far more urgency.

People are losing faith in their leaders and questioning the traditional financial system. Investors have no good places to put their money anymore. Rich people want to protect their wealth against currency devaluation and reckless governments. Businesses need better digital goods and services to prosper in the post-COVID-19 world. Workers suffer from the financial vampire of inflation.

Everybody worries about how long our economic crisis will last, and what will happen to them before it ends.

These are real problems, today.

Cryptocurrency can solve these problems—if we choose to let it.

Perhaps DeFi will get rid of its pyramid schemes, interest-rate shenanigans, and greater fools. Some tokens actually do solve market inefficiencies or present new financial paradigms, they're just mixed in with a bunch of scams, quick-money rug-pulls, and bad ideas.

In time, we will see what works and what doesn't. Trial and error will end the old debates over soft vs. hard money, central banks vs. private money, fiat vs. whatever.

With cryptocurrency, anybody can create a financial system and release it on a global scale. Let's use that power for the benefit of humanity and discovery.

Even better—let's support everybody trying to do so, whether or not they do it with bitcoin.

The money will come

We can do this because we know bitcoin's price *will* go up. The rest of the market *will* follow.

That's not a hope or speculation. It's already happening.

The broad crypto market is up 300% over the past 18 months. Every metric, data point, and historical correlation predicts bitcoin's price will go up for several more years, as it's done since the beginning of 2019.

Does that mean we should expect to reach those lofty numbers people toss around? $1 million bitcoin and 10,000% returns from altcoins?

Maybe. I don't make predictions. I just try to follow the data and try to understand what's a realistic expectation at any given time. An educated guess, based on facts and evidence.

When you look at the data, it's pretty clear a $350,000 bitcoin is far more realistic than a $3,500 bitcoin.

$350k continues the path we've traveled for 11 years. $3.5k nullifies every bit of data, correlation, and pattern we've ever seen relating how people use bitcoin and how its price has moved over its entire history.

Altcoins will follow wherever bitcoin goes. Some will do far better.

Looking ahead

While we owe it to ourselves and our families to think about the wealth-making opportunities in crypto, it's too easy to lose sight of the bigger picture.

In the post-COVID-19 world, where humanity struggles to find its path forward, cryptocurrency will not thrive if its biggest advocates talk *only* about prices and its biggest selling feature is "it goes up."

Think about the true revolution—open, permissionless financial networks that nobody can manipulate, defraud, or deceive.

As bitcoin's price goes up, attention will follow.

Will this renewed attention lead to better, freer, more equitable money systems?

Can we use this moment to make finance and commerce accessible to everybody, not just a lucky few?

Do we harness this momentum to recruit great thinkers and bold leaders who can move this technology into the mainstream?

We can, but only if we choose to.

No matter how gloomy the future seems, humanity always wins. We have an amazing capacity to learn, change, and persist. We embrace new concepts when they make our lives better and reject old concepts when experience shows us a better way.

To succeed, cryptocurrency needs to do only one thing: give humans a better way.

This is the next challenge.

I can't wait to see who accepts it. Relax and enjoy the ride!

October 2020

The U.S. presidential election takes place in a few weeks, marking the first time two people older than 70 will challenge each other for the office.

The world will soon find out who will head its largest economy for the next four years, with ramifications for every country's fortunes.

Some people think the outcome of this election will sway the markets, as in, *all* the markets—stocks, crypto, gold, currencies, bonds, you name it.

I'll believe it when I see it.

Smart money knows presidents have little impact on the economy or any major asset class. The world's economies, stock markets, bond markets, and commodity markets show no correlation to any U.S. political party or president.

In the charts below, I shaded the years of Democratic Party rule in blue. The years of Republican rule have no color.

Can you find any correlations?

GDP

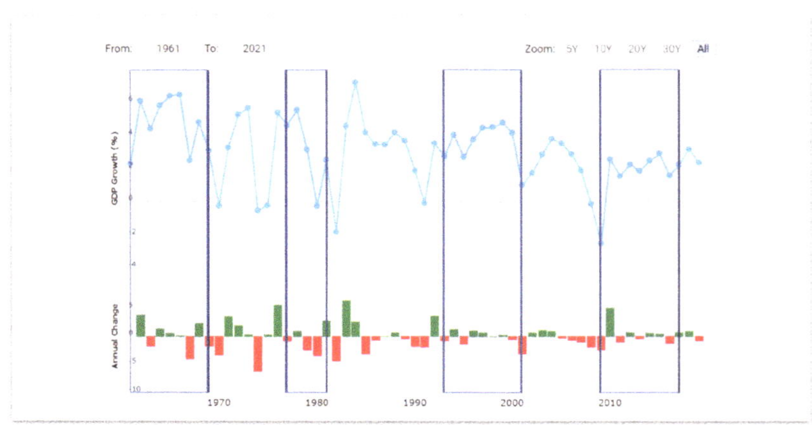

Dow Jones Industrial Average (proxy for stock market)

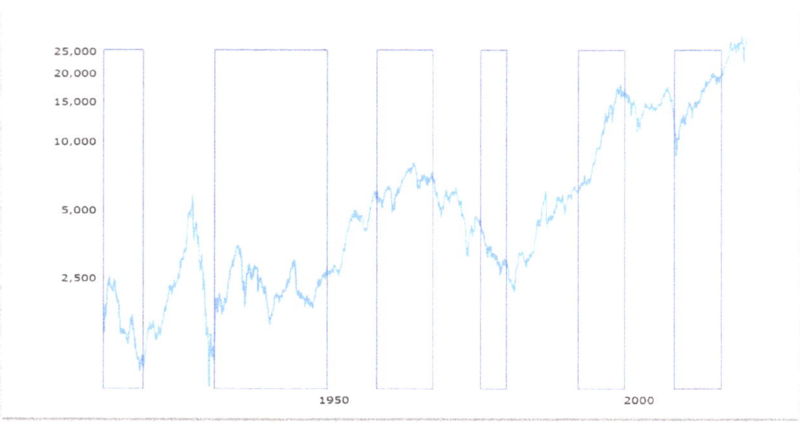

Gold

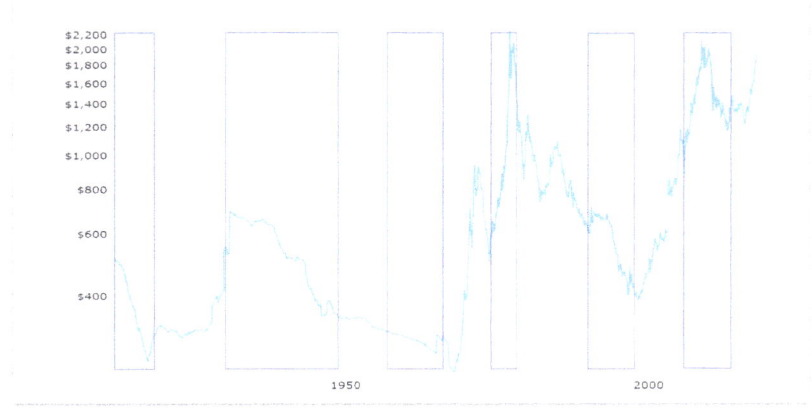

I don't see any. Do you?

Recessions don't correlate to a political party, either.

Look at this image, which overlays recessions (yellow) with political party control over the past 100 years.

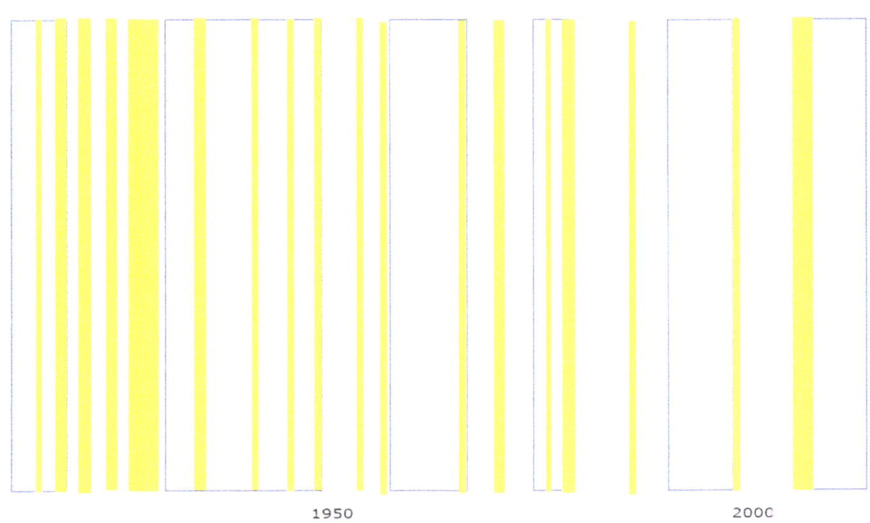

Lots of yellow stripes, regardless of which party holds the presidency.

Yes, in my lifetime, all three recessions have come under Republican administrations.

I suspect this is simply because we've had Republican presidents for more years than Democrats. As a result, Republican presidents have had more chances to get a recession.

If we'd had more years of Democratic presidents, we would have seen more recessions during Democratic administrations. It's not because of political party. It's simply mathematical probability.

Whoever wins this election, the U.S. will continue the path it's been on for decades: more power for the wealthy and well-connected, government programs that lack funding, a patchwork healthcare system, crumbling roads, and schools that taxpayers refuse to pay for—all of it financed by debt and subsidized by workers.

Thus continues an American tradition that may seem completely common in your country, too:

Perpetual disappointment in government, leaders who fail to deliver on their promises, and governments that never seem to do enough—or, depending on your view, always do too much.

Until now (maybe)

Cryptocurrency gives us an alternative to the chaos and conflict of politics.

With cryptocurrency, we don't need to wait for an election or pray our central bankers make the right decisions. Our fate doesn't depend on somebody else's ambitions.

No matter what party holds political power, our blockchains will always do what they're programmed to do. When one stops working, we can move to another, as we might switch car brands or jobs. When whales consolidate power and control over a network, we can abandon them.

When a coordinated few set up roadblocks and competitive moats to exclude us from their prosperity, we will not need to revolt, protest, fight them, or start social movements. We will simply find a different app, a better protocol, or a laptop with a decent internet connection and good computing power from which we can create our own alternative.

Like the rich people and special interests that hold such sway over our politicians, we will get to vote with our money. Our freedom is our choice.

The separation of money and state

Once monetary systems free themselves of government control, we will have a chance to innovate, adapt, and unleash the power of free markets and human ingenuity—or, support those who do, with the expectation we will benefit from their hard work.

As long as we are allowed to do so.

As such, governments have a big role to play. Will they allow this new technology to prosper?

Perhaps we should reflect less on any specific policy and think more about how our leaders feel about financial freedom, privacy, and innovation.

Do they see opportunity in open, permissionless financial networks and trustless, censorship-resistant social organizations?

Will they support financial inclusion at the risk their citizens will switch to a currency that their government doesn't control? Can they envision a world where choice and diversity don't undermine consensus and governance?

Do they want people to exchange goods and services with everybody, not just the people of their own race or nationality?

Assuming you find a politician that does, are you willing to vote for that person if you don't like the political party they're affiliated with?

Change your leaders before Wall Street does it for you

Over the coming decades, today's nascent blockchains will blossom into massive financial networks that capture enormous amounts of value, money, and commerce.

This growth will not happen in a vacuum. Somebody needs to set rules and boundaries, and governments will have to play some role in those decisions.

Traditional finance knows that. These big, special interests don't care about who holds power. They're happy to work with anybody that can get them what they want.

Cryptocurrency will make them obsolete—unless they can get ahead of it and make it their own.

I know nobody in finance who fears cryptocurrency. Some plan to get out with what they can take before cryptos take over. Most want to hop on the train before it leaves the station, and they're happy to let governments help them get where they want to go.

In *Bitcoin or Bust: Wall Street's Entry Into Cryptocurrency*, I discuss many ways they will try to shift the playing field for cryptocurrency in their favor (probably against you).

One way they'll do this is by lobbying governments for laws and regulations that drive money, access, and power into their hands and out of yours. As blockchain technology grows, it will force all of us to make trade-offs between freedom, choice, security, and public welfare.

Everybody wants the good without the bad. Unfortunately, life isn't that easy.

For example, in most countries, financial institutions have to screen or report suspicious transactions. DeFi protocols can't do this—they're just computer codes. Yet, governments still need to investigate and prosecute criminals.

Will they target developers? After all, devs build the platforms and protocols. They have the keys. They control the frontends.

What happens if governments hold developers liable for problems with their code or if somebody uses it for evil purposes? Will this raise barriers to entry and create new risks for anybody trying to innovate—possibly making the costs and risks so high, only a deep-pocketed or well-financed entity can do it? What good is an open, permissionless system if only an elite few have the resources to participate in it?

Sometimes, businesses sponsor this work. Why should they have to follow 50-year-old banking laws and the 80-year-old financial regulations? At no point do they touch their users' money or custody any investment product. How does the public benefit from censorship-resistant, private financial networks if anybody can cut us off from accessing them?

If you own a DeFi governance token, operate a node, stake or delegate to validators, can governments hold *you* responsible if the platform breaks the law? You didn't have anything to do with that, you simply joined the network. And yet, you own a part of that network and a voice in its decisions. Should government expect you to know every section of the legal code—and every way your decentralized, leaderless organization broke it?

Or, do regulators throw their hands up and say "everybody needs to use a custodial wallet from a registered financial institution because it's the only way we can regulate the industry" and let the banks and other traditional financial institutions corner the market.

Do governments force their citizens to turn over private keys? Use licenses, registrations, and certifications to limit who can develop cryptocurrencies?

Hate government at your own risk

When you argue about fiat vs. bitcoin, traditional finance laughs. It's happy to make money on both.

With so many ways for powerful, well-connected players to steer crypto into their hands, I'm amazed how many people still worry about crypto bans.

Don't fear the bans. Those never work.

Fear the lobbyists. They *always* work.

Somebody needs to create the tax laws, privacy protections, intellectual property frameworks, and regulatory structures that govern what people do with cryptocurrency, even if only to say "nobody can torture you for your private keys."

Each decision creates an opportunity for somebody to screw you over.

Today's conversations revolve around monetary authority and the particulars of securities laws.

This is no longer tenable. The pace of innovation is too fast. The spread of novel applications is too swift.

Facebook was easy to intimidate. It's a big corporation with lots of money at stake.

Random Joe's altcoin project is not. Its team is spread across several continents. Its investors are anonymous and the work happens in obscurity—until one day, a Tweet or Medium post sparks a rally.

There are thousands of Random Joes working on altcoin projects. Some will deliver amazing products and services that challenge the boundaries of law and finance.

And no government will be able to stop them. Governments rule over people. Cryptocurrencies are not people. They're protocols. DAOs and source codes.

For those who say the industry will police itself or competition will lead to better governance, I suggest taking a little deeper interest in history and psychology.

Cryptocurrencies are usually scarce assets and blockchains compete in a zero-sum game. What do people do with scarce assets and zero-sum games?

Fight, compete, and screw each other over.

For every Jack Dorsey, there's a Roger Ver. For every Caitlin Long, there's a John McAfee.

If government is inevitable, let's have *good* government. Let's advocate for freedom, not profits. Goods and services, not capital gains.

We know the money will come. We don't need to flaunt it.

Instead, let's push for sane rules, shared goals, and fair playing fields. Let's find opportunities for cryptocurrency to serve the public's welfare.

We need to make sure our legacy is not BitMex, Mt. Gox, and Lambos.

The more we can do that—advocate for freedom, choice, fairness, empowerment, and access to financial opportunities—the less it matters who wins this, or any, election. Some human values transcend politics.

A movement without political affiliation

For that reason, I'm writing in my vote this year. I will vote for bitcoin.

Until a leader shows me they care about any of the values we stand for, I can't give him or her my vote. At least bitcoin has my back.

Is that a cop-out?

No.

Those who understand the U.S. political system know some states are so overwhelmingly partisan, one candidate is all but guaranteed to win its presidential votes. I live in one of those states. My vote for president doesn't matter.

I have the luxury of voting my conscience.

Does that mean I think government actions will keep cryptocurrency prices from going up?

No, quite the opposite. Those actions will make people think crypto's legit. Nobody kicks a dead dog.

In turn, people will find it easier to justify participating and investing. This will lead to more growth, awareness, positivity, and traction. It will build a strong social foundation for the growth that comes after this next market cycle peak, once the gains are made and lost.

I only hope those gains go to people who truly need it, and those losses affect only those who can afford it.

At some point, politics may matter for cryptocurrency's fate. Today, we need only worry about the values our leaders bring to government service.

If we do that, everything else will take care of itself.

Economic recovery: reality or mirage?

Meanwhile, economies continue to struggle and COVID-19 seems to never end.

Perhaps all is not as bad as it seems.

Despite a steady stream of news reports lamenting second waves and new lockdowns, some of the world's economies have seen recent growth.

For example, this past quarter, U.S. GDP grew possibly as high as 14% on an annualized basis. Unemployment dropped, as did personal savings, showing people and businesses have started to gain confidence in their financial situations.

China logged an 11% annualized growth rate. In many countries, the pace of decline has slowed or reversed totally. People are getting jobs again. Markets are finding new efficiencies and opportunities to grow.

All signs point to recovery.

Yet, it seems absurd to expect our economies will continue to go up.

Over 30% of U.S. households are behind on rent. More than 60% of businesses plan to downsize office space *regardless of whether or not they make more money.* Huge segments of the economy remain closed. Businesses are failing at the highest rate in 12 years.

Nobody talks about debt markets that are still out-of-whack, millions of people living check-to-check, billions of dollars locked in zombie corporations, trillions of dollars in bad debt sitting on central bank balance sheets, the looming end to government-imposed deferrals of rents and mortgages, a near-collapse of commercial real estate markets, and the total destruction of safe, income-generating investments.

Maybe we didn't give ourselves enough credit? Perhaps we were too resilient and adaptable.

We have lots of amazing people fighting to keep our economies afloat and so many proactive, enterprising people fighting for their financial lives—and ours.

Maybe they're succeeding?

Light at the end of the pandemic tunnel

Some say we will have another global lockdown because COVID-19 infection rates have shot up pretty much everywhere. Recently, several countries have imposed new restrictions.

As alarming as this seems, I can't imagine these measures will last very long. Flare-ups will continue until people consistently wear masks, wash hands, and avoid close social contact.

Our standards of care and medical countermeasures have improved a lot since the beginning of this year.

When COVID-19 started, lockdowns were pretty much the only effective response.

Today, everything has changed. We know how to stop the disease from spreading and we can better screen for symptoms, trace contacts, and test effectively.

Also, while infection rates have gone up in recent days, those infections have led to fewer deaths and faster recoveries in almost every country.

Perhaps this is because milder COVID-19 strains have replaced the deadlier ones? Researchers have found some evidence of that.

More likely, it's because we're so much better at testing, tracking, and treating COVID-19.

U.S. President Trump serves as a great example of how far we've come in our fight.

Thanks to better standards of care, improved testing, and experimental drugs, he survived a case of COVID-19 so severe that his doctors had to give him a course of treatment normally reserved for people about to die. The people he infected had a chance to quarantine and distance from others. For the contacts who needed medical care, they had a chance to seek treatment before their symptoms got worse.

The president went back to work after five days.

Six months ago this incident could have led to a super-spreader outbreak that immobilized the U.S. government—or worse.

Today, it sends a few people to the hospital and forces the others to stay home for two weeks.

Vaccine research progresses at a rapid pace and we have several promising treatments that could enter the market soon.

As somebody who works for the U.S. government agency responsible for COVID-19 research, I think most people will be surprised at how quickly the world's governments, pharmaceutical companies, and public health organizations will move once we know what works and what doesn't.

I'll bet we'll have the information we need by the end of this year.

How long will it take to get the right treatments into the hands of enough people to end this pandemic?

Months, probably.

To some, this sounds like an eternity. To others, it seems too soon.

Either way, we will soon move the global bastard from "urgent pandemic" to "one of many diseases that sometimes kill people."

Then, life will go back to normal.

Prepare for what comes next

Things can change in an instant, but in the big picture, the overall trend looks positive on all fronts.

What does this mean for cryptocurrency? Does it really follow the stock market? Will we get another crash, a global depression, and a deflationary cycle? More BRRRR from central banks? Stimulus checks deposited into bitcoin ATMs and Coinbase accounts?

I'm still not convinced crypto markets have any correlation to the real economy or any government stimulus.

The world's governments printed trillions of dollars and barely a fraction of a percent went into the cryptocurrency markets. Cryptocurrency exchange inflows and outflows show no relationship to GDP growth or government spending. Almost 2/3 of all bitcoins haven't moved in a year.

Of all the correlations people throw out to explain bitcoin's price movements, the U.S. dollar is the strongest I've seen yet. When USD goes up, bitcoin goes down. When USD goes down, bitcoin goes up. We've seen this pattern for years.

Guess what?

USD continues to fall.

Whether the world's economies recover quickly or plunge into a global depression—or anywhere in between—USD will probably continue to fall.

Some economists think that USD's fall will help the world's economies recover from COVID-19. It makes emerging market debt easier to finance, lowers international barriers to commodity markets, and encourages U.S. consumers to buy locally as the prices of foreign imports rise.

Complacency kills

As great as the big picture looks, with all the big trends pointing up, we can't get ahead of ourselves. We remain stuck in a financial crisis, a pandemic outbreak, and an economic downturn.

That's today's reality.

When you look around, it may seem like everything's stable. Hell, bitcoin's up 50% on the year.

Still, I can't help but worry. It's not rational for so much positive data to come in such a dismal environment.

So . . . buy bitcoin now?

That's the question I get the most.

We are so far from the market cycle peak, there's no reason to think about that.

Every price is a good price. Where we're headed, you won't care whether you bought at $10,000 or $12,000. If anything, you will regret not buying more at either price.

Does that mean we should buy cryptocurrency only when prices go down?

No.

It does mean we should avoid chasing the pumps and keep some money on-hand to buy the dips.

Stay the course

My investment thesis on bitcoin has not changed, nor have I seen any data to suggest it should. Bitcoin's price always goes up and it works when the financial system doesn't.

Some altcoins will outperform bitcoin.

All of the long-term drivers of value remain strong and the data points in one direction for crypto prices over the long-term:

Up.

Everybody I know on the inside says money from family offices and portfolio managers is coming in by the truckload, from all directions. HODL waves show OGs and whales are accumulating bitcoin like crazy. VCs are inking deals like it's 2017 again.

At the same time, traditional investment assets have lost their yields and gained new risks, making crypto look comparatively more attractive.

With so much positive momentum in our favor, we just need to commit to the market.

This should be easy—after all, the prices are low, the upside is high, and the technology is developing at a rapid pace.

Yet, I see your emails and read the comments in my WhatsApp and Telegram chats. For too many of us, it's not easy.

I hope my analysis and content make it a little easier. This analysis and content will get more and more valuable as the markets rise, your investments go up, and your emotions get stronger.

As you have more money to lose with each market swing, it's natural to worry.

Everything will get harder

Once we get closer to the market cycle peak, you will worry more.

I realize some of you will not be subscribed to this newsletter once we get to that point, but that's really when you're going to need it the most. Follow my plan, and this market is easy.

Did you find it hard to buy bitcoin when its price crashed below $10,000? Did you feel anxious when its price started going up again?

If you found it hard to handle a move from $9k to $12.5k to $10k over three months, just wait until we go from $90k to $125k to $100k *in three weeks.*

Have you ever lost $20,000 in a week?

You might struggle to resist the urge to "take profits" and "sell the local top," even though I will wait until we see very specific, time-tested signals that the market's getting near its peak.

On the flip side, imagine how hard it will be to sell once we do get near the market cycle peak, when everybody else is getting in, feeling great, and making fast money. Your portfolio may double or triple in a month. And then, seemingly out of nowhere, I will tell you to sell.

Just when everybody else is *finally* on board.

It will be the right decision.

The next time prices hit those levels, smart money, OGs, and Wall Street will crash the market and run off with your family's wealth.

(We have data on that, too.)

You need to protect yourself.

If you think losing a few hundred bucks on a DeFi rug-pull hurts, imagine how bad it will feel when insiders, early investors, investment firms, and so-called champions like Square and MicroStrategy start yanking billions of dollars out of the markets all at once.

Do you have the courage to sell when *everybody else* tells you you're crazy and it seems like prices will do nothing but go up forever?

You'll have to.

In the future, not now

Today, we don't have to think about that. We're lucky.

We're invested in this market when there's no bad time to buy and no price too high (except for dead coins and DeFi pump-and-dumps).

For that reason, I'm not upset that during this most recent crash, I only invested 22% of the money that I had set aside for it. Just one of the hazards of averaging into the market. Statistically, you're supposed to get more value from that approach, but it doesn't always work out that way. That's ok.

There will be more dips along the way, possibly worse than the one we just had, and possibly a continuation of it. I'll keep my cash in my Celsius account at 11% interest and wait for the next opportunity.

If you're thinking about selling, keep in mind: every time you sell your cryptocurrency, you give away your stake in the financial networks of the future.

Perhaps you'll have a chance to buy in at a lower price—but if that's the case, why not just add to your stack when we reach that lower price? Do you have no other source of income? No other reserve to pull cash into the market? Is crypto your only hope of making money?

If so, you may want to use this time to think about your finances. That's not easy, either—but it's easier than guessing which direction crypto prices will go.

We may *never* reach another market cycle peak. It's possible crypto will either die or continue to grow naturally, organically, in measured steps, without another speculative bubble.

How many years can you stay invested in this market under those circumstances? Are you willing to wait a decade to find out whether your favorite altcoin is really the next bitcoin?

Those are probably rhetorical questions.

More likely, we will continue to see prices, interest, and innovation rise while governments largely ignore us. Pro-crypto special interests will continue bending the right ears and throwing money at the right politicians. Economies will recover, slowly, with a lot of pain and hardship for too many people. COVID-19 will join the long list of tragedies that humans have overcome.

And these young financial networks will grow to such scale and value, you will look back on this moment and wonder what you were ever worried about.

Relax and enjoy the ride!

November 2020

Congratulations! Bitcoin's nearing all-time highs and altcoins have started to follow. Everything's going to plan.

Let's look beyond the day-to-day and focus on what really matters—things far more important than a 70% pump in bitcoin's price.

But first, a question: where is the great depression?

After nine months of financial crisis and pandemic disease, aren't we supposed to be in worldwide economic freefall with massive inflation? Especially with new COVID-19 restrictions in some countries. Why hasn't unemployment killed more people than COVID-19?

Instead, we have shrinking unemployment in many places, along with growth and record profits for many segments of the economy in many parts of the world, even in some places that have tamped down on social gatherings and high-risk activities or seen big spikes in hospitalizations.

While that's no comfort to you if you're living under lockdowns or worried about your job, life, or business, it's the present reality. Much of the world has started to recover. Hopefully, you will, too.

"

Has anything really changed since March?

Debt markets are still out of whack. Government debt keeps piling up. Many people are again living with lockdowns and curfews.

In the U.S., COVID-19 outbreaks have put so many people in hospitals in some parts of the country, their schools and businesses have had to shut down voluntarily (too many workers sick and dying). Supply chain disruptions have started winding their way through the economy, resulting in backlogs, shortages, and higher prices for many goods.

Government assistance for unprofitable businesses, delinquent tenants, and mortgage holders will soon end. About 30% of businesses and households are late on their rent payments. Business bankruptcies remain near record levels and many economists predict personal bankruptcy rates will skyrocket as governments lift financial protections and medical costs go up. Rents in big city centers have crashed.

Maybe it's like that where you live?

I realize nobody talks about these things anymore, because the stock markets have recovered and home values are rising.

It's amazing how people's perspectives change when prices go up.

Do you realize nobody's really fixed any of the underlying problems that caused the financial crisis in the first place? We just printed money and hoped the markets would work everything out.

Perhaps that was enough?

Think out of both sides of your head

Lockdowns will end. We have a vaccine and at least one more on the way, with several treatments ready for mass production. Asset prices continue to rise. Businesses have started growing again (in many cases, they never shrunk).

At every moment, so many things can go wrong, but humanity remains creative, talented, resilient, industrious, and persistent.

Markets adjust. People cope.

We endure.

If you want crypto to succeed, the recovery *must* continue. Crypto Twitter and bitcoin maximalists may disagree. I'm sure they still have plenty of reasons to see doom in the financial system and this nascent economic recovery. BRRR, bubbles, banks, all that.

Of course, it's hard to tell because every Tweet is about the price or how some Wall Street guy bought bitcoin.

It's amazing how people's perspectives change when prices go up.

Still, I suspect they believe what they have always believed: the traditional financial system is bankrupt, bloated, and destined to collapse. Now, we wait for the other shoe to fall. Hyperinflation, where are ye?

True, the traditional financial system might yet fail, but nobody seems to care anymore. Bitcoin's going to the moon!

But COVID-19 . . .

Yes, COVID-19.

Some economies are growing under COVID-19, others are shrinking. Some people lost jobs and businesses, others found new careers and record profits. Some countries prospered despite oppressive mask mandates, soul-killing social distancing, costly expansions of hospital capacity, and expensive, invasive "test, trace, and treat" strategies. Other countries still struggle despite doing none of those things.

Imagine a fire ripped through your neighborhood. Every house caught fire. Some burned down, others didn't. Some homeowners rebuilt and repaired, others did not.

At what point do you start to wonder why only some houses burned down and only some homeowners rebuilt them? When do you start to question whether the fire's really what's keeping you down?

Did you know that in the U.S., the manufacturing sector spent all of 2019 in a recession? Real wages were flat since 2016? A trade war with China was crushing exporters?

Did you know the Fed started flooding the system with money as early as fall 2019 with interventions in obscure parts of the financial system like the repo and short-term bond markets? Google "QE lite." Or that overall growth had started going south by February?

All that was happening *before* any lockdowns.

Makes you wonder what else people weren't talking about because everybody looked at the stock market and thought "best economy ever."

COVID-19 or not, money always goes wherever it can get the best returns.

Pandemic countermeasures drive money and investment into businesses that support those responses. Delivery, takeout, and remote services thrive. People migrate to activities they can do with masks, or intentionally avoid masks totally and spend money on other things. Consumers buy more household goods and subscriptions to streaming platforms.

Some lose, some win.

Cruel, perhaps, but inevitable.

Small consolation for everybody suffering under curfews and stay-at-home orders. Even worse for those hospitalized and dead from COVID-19.

This will get better soon.

Of course, the moment bitcoin crashes again, or the stock market drops, or some bad economic news comes out, people will start blaming COVID-19. Half the people will say governments didn't do enough, the other half will say governments did too much.

As an investor, none of that matters.

New investment paradigm

I'll let the economic historians have the final say on COVID-19's impact. Time will tell whether massive, coordinated, unprecedented government interventions saved the system or delayed its inevitable collapse.

(PS—buy bitcoin so you're protected either way.)

One consequence is clear:

Central banks and governments destroyed the value of safe, low-risk assets. In doing so, they created a new investment paradigm.

Cash yields nothing (and sometimes costs you money). Most bonds can't cover the rate of inflation. Bonds that do cover inflation come with a high risk of default. Corporations have slashed dividends. P/E ratios have skyrocketed. IPOs now fetch outlandish valuations they can't possibly sustain over the long term.

When you account for risk, *every asset has a poor expected return on investment.*

True, if the dollar continues to fall, you can make good risk-adjusted returns in emerging market debt and commodity markets. And investment properties always deliver great returns if you know how to manage real estate. But few people have access to those investments or know how to use them (and I'm not sure you ever want to bet against the U.S. dollar over the long term).

On the flip side, U.S. investment firms have $26 trillion in assets under management and U.S. households have more than $18 trillion in cash, savings, and money market accounts.

A similar situation exists in other countries, too, albeit on a smaller scale.

On top of that, global funds, foreign investors, and offshore accounts hold upwards of $40 trillion. Nobody knows how much sits in corporate treasuries and business reserves.

So far, that money has mostly NOT gone into crypto. Of the $10 trillion in new money governments printed earlier this year, less than .1% entered the crypto markets.

Guess what's changed since then?

Nothing.

Except prices have gone up for a while.

In fact, cryptocurrency returns have far outpaced those of every other asset class.

No wonder institutional investors, rich people, and a few corporations have started putting some money into bitcoin. Nobody has the patience and discipline to continue losing money with cash, stocks, gold, and bonds while bitcoin's price explodes.

At some point, once altcoins get large and liquid enough for big money to buy in any substantial amount, these same investors will add some exposure to the alts.

They will do this because that's how humans think about money.

It's amazing how people's perspectives change when prices go up.

While Google's search data for cryptocurrency suggest normal people haven't noticed yet, they will soon. Rich people and insiders have made it seem safe, entrepreneurs have made it easy to access, governments have made it regulated and legitimate, and bitcoin's price has made new highs.

We have all the ingredients for a massive boom.

Traditional assets have more risks and less upside than ever before, while cryptocurrency has *fewer* risks and *more* upside than ever before.

Where do you think people will put their money?

Remember the investment thesis

Still, we can't get ahead of ourselves. For the same reason we need to stay grounded as prices rise, we need to make sure we have a clear investment thesis.

In the short run, *any asset's price can go up*, sometimes for much longer than you expect.

That doesn't mean it's a good investment or a good time to buy.

One trick I learned from studying how professionals invest: always have an investment thesis, a reason to expect prices will go up in the future.

For example, my investment thesis for bitcoin is simple: price always goes up and it works when the financial system doesn't. Factually correct, easy to prove, easy to understand.

If that seems too simple, you're probably right. When you have compelling evidence, facts, data, and history on an asset and its technology, you don't need to complicate things.

I also happen to believe everybody should have a source of wealth and a way to do business that doesn't depend on the traditional financial system. Good luck getting anybody to agree with me :-)

What's *your* investment thesis?

Geeze, Mark, always about bitcoin. What about altcoins?

Right, altcoins. Everybody wants every altcoin to go back to its all-time high yesterday.

Cryptocurrency is the only asset class where investors get disappointed about 500% returns. It's the only market where you can triple your money in a matter of weeks, suffer a 50% market crash in a matter of days, then go up another 6x a few months later . . . and still feel like you lost money.

As long as you stay smart and disciplined, the gains will come. Volume and price will continue to grow. Long-term patterns have started to signal a shift in momentum from bitcoin to altcoins.

I've shared the specific data with premium subscribers and won't get into it here, but the data is very clear about what's happening in the altcoin market once you dig beneath the hype and look beyond the daily price swings.

The alts may seem subdued because lots of people lost money in DeFi and lots of altcoins have inflationary tokenomics, which means their token prices don't necessarily rise as their market caps grow.

Don't let appearances fool you.

Cryptocurrency won the presidential election

You may think the U.S. election is under dispute.

It's not.

The president's team claims fraud and tweets all sorts of evidence, but they don't present any of that evidence in court. Even their "independent advisors" found no fraud.

They really should put up or shut up. Let the lawsuits and recounts proceed, present the evidence, find out the truth, and if there is any fraud, deal with it in accordance with the law.

So far, all the suits have been thrown out or tackled minor points of law, for example, the scope of election officials' responsibilities, how closely somebody needs to stand next to a ballot-counter to be considered an "observer," whether to accept ballots filled out with permanent marker, things like that.

After recounts and audits, you can expect we'll find mistakes. That happens with every election. If you listen to the people who do this stuff for a living, those mistakes cancel each other out. Some in favor of one candidate, some in favor of the other.

Will we find enough mistakes to change the results?

We shall see.

Given Trump is now raising money for his next campaign, I get the sense even he accepts the result, despite his public statements. Either that or he's ripping off his contributors and supporters.

Since it's Trump, you never know—but it's never a good sign when your Secretary of State has to stifle a laugh when talking about a transition to your second term.

Bottom line: unless something changes drastically, the U.S. will have a new president in January.

What does this mean for crypto?

Considering the Trump administration's public and well-documented disdain for cryptocurrency, I would expect a new administration to take a more favorable view. Not sure it could get any worse.

Keep in mind, presidents don't make laws. That's Congress's job. U.S. regulations come from financial laws that are 50 to 86 years old. Until the laws change, there's not much any president can do about cryptocurrency. He can issue regulatory approvals and guidance, perhaps a few executive orders. Significant actions but hardly game-changers.

So it really depends on how much emphasis the new administration puts on cryptocurrency and pushing Congress for crypto legislation.

That's a realistic possibility. Some of the new president's biggest donors have strong ties to crypto. Silicon Valley has a lot of influence in Democratic Party circles and Wall Street has its hands in both parties' pockets.

If you believe the rumors about who Biden will appoint as cabinet officials and top advisors, you will find a slew of pro-crypto, pro-blockchain appointees.

Bitcoin ETF, anybody? Safe harbor for small investors? Sane tax guidance and regulations? Money for blockchain projects? Those things are a lot more likely with this administration than the outgoing one.

Also, the Democratic Party skews younger, both in absolute numbers and as a proportion of people who register as Democrats compared to Republicans. Many surveys show young people have more positive opinions of cryptocurrency than old people.

If we're speculating on hypotheticals, I can imagine an interesting dynamic could play out within the Democratic Party. This party has a lot of pro-Wall Street people and a lot of anti-Wall Street people. The pro-Wall Street people want institutional and government involvement to clean up the cryptocurrency industry and let them make money from it, while the anti-Wall Street people think cryptocurrency can destroy what they see as an unfair system that rewards rich people for ripping off poor people and small businesses.

Maybe they'll find kindred spirits with Republicans who value free markets, individual liberties, small government, and low taxes. As a result, the U.S. will finally get sensible cryptocurrency laws.

Or not. It's fun to speculate.

In any event, cryptocurrency is a bipartisan issue—namely, neither party cares about it much. It may rise in prominence as the market attracts more investment and prices go up, but it's anybody's guess how Washington will respond.

Will Biden lock down the U.S.?

We'll see.

Until January 20, 2021, Biden can't do anything. A lot can change in two months.

Whatever happens, I doubt it will affect crypto. The entire market doubled during our previous lockdown and big money gobbled up tons of bitcoin. It continues to rise despite lockdowns in some parts of the world and new restrictions in some parts of the U.S.

I can't see why another lockdown would get a different result.

Let's hope we don't have to find out.

Plan ahead and stick to the plan

While everything seems like the stars are aligning for crypto, many still struggle to make ends meet. The recovery is fragile. Government support programs will expire soon. Probably 1/3 of people will refuse to take a COVID-19 vaccine, and even if they do, we have a long way to go before we get back to normal.

None of that seems to matter for crypto.

For the past twelve years, we have seen certain patterns and correlations repeat regardless of the global financial, economic, or political situation.

We can't predict the future, but we can use this data to prepare for the most realistic outcomes.

All those outcomes point in one direction: Up.

Avoid the shillers

Nobody can always buy at the absolute lowest price at all times, no matter what they tell you.

You can't worry about the price. Focus on the opportunity.

As long as we get in before the pumps, we don't have to stress about them or worry about the crashes. We don't have to check prices and charts all day because we know our investments will go up over time. And, since we know in advance when the bull market will end, so we can get out with as much of our wealth as possible.

If you missed this zoom, another opportunity will come soon, and it will be an opportunity of a lifetime. You don't want to miss it.

See with your mind, not your eyes

In the short run, anything can happen.

In the long run, certain patterns and trends always play out the same way. In fact, they're often so compelling, you can't deny them—even though others will.

Today, we have the highest bitcoin price in years, continuous growth in altcoins (prices and technology), a positive macro-economic environment, a traditional financial system increasingly unable to deliver the returns people expect, tons of money sitting in bank accounts and underperforming investment funds, and a COVID-19 vaccine (with more coming by the end of this year).

Fundamentally, *nothing* has changed in the past six months. Same risks, same opportunities.

It sure feels different, though—doesn't it?

It's amazing how people's perspectives change when prices go up.

Who knows what will happen tomorrow? Are you prepared for a massive crash?

What about all the other risks? This is a speculative market built on technology that hasn't found any mainstream applications yet. Most people still believe it's a fad, scam, and destined to fail. Some governments want to crush it or take it from their people.

You dream about 5,000% returns. In this market, those returns are not only possible, *they are realistic.*

But you will never get all of that.

Nobody buys the absolute low and sells the absolute high.

Sometimes, it's OK to plan for a few outcomes, then take it as it comes. You can't stress about every up and down or obsess about every swing in prices. You can't get upset about ***only*** a 1,000% return.

We know this market is going up. Everything else is just details: the best tokens to buy, the best time to buy, the best time to sell, and how to go about it so you have the best chance of getting the most value from those decisions.

Those details can change in a flash. To pretend you or anybody else can keep up with all the changes in this market? Foolish.

Appreciate this moment

As prices rise, you may feel like you should've put more money when prices were lower.

No matter how much you put into the market, *it will never feel like it's enough*.

It's ok to feel good about what you already have invested. You can use your good fortune for other investments, or perhaps start a business or some other way to build wealth and boost your financial fortunes.

Remember that old stock market adage: bulls get fed, bears get fed, pigs get slaughtered.

Reality usually does not change when prices do. No opportunity this massive comes without equally massive risks.

Don't sweat the dips, don't FOMO the pumps, and find really good altcoins (not "safe" large caps that aren't really safe).

There are a lot of things to worry about. Look at the bright side: in the midst of pandemic disease, political uncertainty, and economic distress, you have the time, money, and good fortune to buy a stake in the financial networks of the future—and get rewarded for doing so.

We have so much to look forward to.

Relax and enjoy the ride!

December 2020

A few days ago, bitcoin blasted past its previous all-time high and tapped $24,000.

Old friends started texting you about crypto again, for the first time in years. *Wall Street Journal* started reporting on bitcoin.

Bitcoin maximalists stopped talking about how "bitcoin fixes this" and started mocking gold bugs and talking about how much money they're going to make selling their bitcoin for "fiat."

Everybody says there are no more bitcoins left to sell. Institutions are buying straight from the miners because nobody's selling through the exchanges and OTC desks. Technical analysis on trading charts show lines going up and triangles pointing in bullish directions.

Smells like 2017 all over again, right?

Better yet, the U.S. government will soon print another $900 billion and flood the world with *even more dollars* on top of the trillions it printed earlier this year.

Are you ready for the ride of your life?

I sure hope so.

To get a great first-person view of the agony and ecstasy of the 2016-2017 bull market, buy Dan Conway's fun book,

Confessions of a Cryptocurrency Millionaire, so you're in the right mental state.

For now, enjoy the holiday season and if you practice a different religion or you're not into religion at all, take it easy and reflect on the good things you have.

In this month's issue, I'll talk about the transition from smart money and institutional investors to retail buyers and the general public.

People are catching up to us

Since the day I created this newsletter, I have talked about the importance of patience and letting others come around to what's going on. Facts and data usually don't change people's minds, they mostly confirm what people already want to believe.

This market will take off when bitcoin's price goes up long enough for people to believe it will keep going up.

Some say it just did. They said that in July 2019 too—and we know how that turned out.

(Bad. Nine months of prices going down in a slow bleed.)

I doubt we will get that same outcome, but let's not get ahead of ourselves. Big moves are the norm in this market.

If rumors, tweets, and my friends' text messages are true, Aunt Sally and Uncle Morton finally put a little money into bitcoin and some large cap altcoins.

Not much, of course. Just nibbles. Testing the waters, or, for some, getting back into the pool after a long time out of the water.

It'll take a little longer before they start moving serious money into the markets.

With Grayscale, PayPal, Square, Bitwise, Bakkt, banks, and other companies eager to make money from their interest in crypto, you can bet you'll see more advertisements, promotions, and media placements. Everything will seem safe and fun.

"Only risk money you can afford to lose, of course, but buy now. You may never get another chance!"

Does that make your toes tingle and your heart flutter?

How would you feel if I told you this latest pump is just a tiny glimpse of what we have to look forward to?

As premium subscribers know, bitcoin's price has gone a little too high, a little too fast for its own good. The market wasn't ready for such a powerful move.

Ideally, we would've cooled off at about $16,000. Since we didn't, it's now only a question of whether the market will catch up to the price before it falls, and what bitcoin's price will be when that happens.

It's all good, though. There's never a bad time to buy bitcoin, it's just that some times are better than others. For altcoins, they're so volatile and we have little historical data, so you might as well average into them no matter what bitcoin's doing.

Bottom line: in the short run, nothing should phase you.

Aim higher

While these past two weeks may seem like an explosion of interest in crypto, I'd encourage you to think much, much bigger.

This little pump only scratches the surface of what we have to look forward to over the next year or two (or three???)

This world has massive amounts of money searching for yield:

- More than $19 trillion in cash, savings, and money market accounts for U.S. households alone. When you include savings from people in other countries, that amount goes much higher.
- Over $26 trillion in U.S.-registered investment funds.
- More than $100 trillion in global government debt.
- Over $200 trillion in corporate and household debt.
- At least $400 trillion in financial products like derivatives and collateralized loan obligations.
- Hundreds of trillions of dollars in real assets like property, cars, and collectibles.

With DeFi platforms, crypto investment products, custody services, banking and insurance infrastructure, and innovations in blockchain technology, *every penny can get tokenized, recorded on a blockchain, and exchanged using cryptocurrency.*

With all that we have to look forward to, you're excited about a $20,000 bitcoin and an altcoin market that's still 50% below its previous all-time high?

Just wait. You ain't seen nothing yet.

From smart money to institutional investors

In the classic anatomy of a bubble chart, market cycles start with smart money and end with the general public. In between, prices explode.

It looks like this:

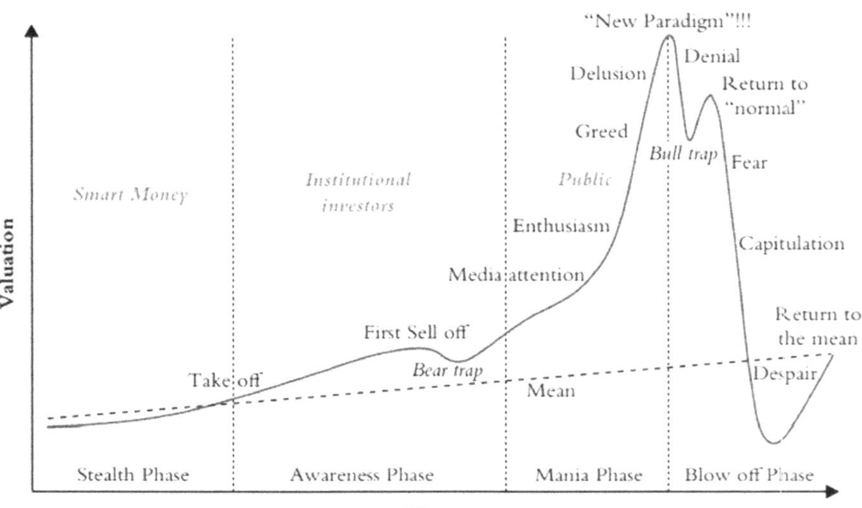

Smart money enters first.

That's you and everybody else who's been in this space for a while. We are the innovators, entrepreneurs, and individual investors who put our money into the market for all the right reasons. We saw the potential, understood the value, and took the time and effort to get in—even though it wasn't a popular decision.

Next comes institutional investors—i.e., Wall Street, VCs, corporations, pensions, and big financial companies. Sometimes they buy assets for themselves, sometimes for clients and speculators. They're looking to get in on "the next big thing." While they might believe in crypto, they really just want to make money.

Next comes the general public, who mostly doesn't care or believe in crypto, they just want a piece of the action.

That's when everything goes crazy.

We're getting close to that shift from institutions to the public.

Perhaps we'll have that big sell-off / bear trap first? Or maybe that happened in March and we will continue big moves up with relatively small crashes along the way?

As we move through this transition into the next phase of the market cycle, only the strong hands will survive. Everybody else will either lose money, give up, or learn how to succeed in this market.

Regardless, the biggest gains will go to those who ignore the random three-week pump of some new DeFi token or FOMO into the latest shill they read on Telegram or Reddit.

Strong hands buy when it seems nobody else is buying—expecting the price to go lower and knowing it's the right decision to move in. They will sit on their hands when it seems like everybody's buying—knowing the price will go up and knowing it's the right decision to sit out.

They won't get excited about buying 10% dips because they will have already bought the +25% crashes, and they will enjoy the pumps because they will have already caught the most recent bottom.

We are those people.

As long as we predominate the market, prices will go up. We will have money to buy when the market falls, raising the floor for prices. We will cool down the greed and delusion that always comes before the market cycle peaks, delaying the inevitable mania so the market can keep rising higher, longer, and stronger than anybody expects.

If we can do that, we will make new buyers feel comfortable with this market—and the money they put into it.

That way, they won't stop at a $500 or $1,000 Coinbase deposit "just to see what this bit-currency thing is all about."

Instead, they will commit good money to it. Financial institutions, insurance companies, and securities issuers will dabble with DeFi platforms and decentralized exchanges. Commercial investment funds will make small investments in pre-sale tokens or buy Aragon's or Theta's tokens for access to those platforms.

MicroStrategy, MassMutual, and Square won't be the only businesses that announce they've put bitcoin into their treasuries.

All of them will.

Markets gonna do what markets gonna do

But nothing goes up in a straight line forever. Either the market crashes or it stalls out long enough to shake out the weak hands, fake believers, and speculators. Then we can sustain those rising prices for the long-term.

Traders love the swings because they can make a lot of money from changes in prices.

As investors, we want massive gains, durable wealth, and incredible windfalls, not 30% swing trades or 2x pumps. That means we depend on others to put their time, money, and faith into the assets we own.

For that reason, we need people to see prices go up long enough for people to believe they will keep going up.

Markets move fast, people don't. When markets move too fast, people can't keep up.

You'd think they'd FOMO in—and some do—but most get spooked. When something's too good to be true, it usually is. Or the market crashes before they can buy. Or they get scammed. Or whatever.

When all you care about is making money from the price of bitcoin going up, what will you do once the price goes down?

As anybody still HODLing a DeFi token from July can attest, you won't buy more.

Once prices go up, everything changes. There are no facts too outlandish for people to believe when they want to feel good about their money. Any justification will do.

And yet, as prices rise, nothing fundamentally changes. Bitcoin did not change as its price went from $10,000 to $24,000.

All is how it was. Progress and price never move in sync.

What matters most?

Trends. Momentum. The bigger picture.

Let the traders worry about prices. We're here for the opportunities.

Smart money always wins

Anybody who has subscribed to *Crypto is Easy* for long enough will have bought bitcoin and altcoins when bitcoin's price was between $5,400 to $7,800, and then again when its price was between $9,800 to $10,100.

We had the courage to invest when it seemed like everything would fall apart—knowing full well it could have done so. We had the patience to wait for the markets to push prices higher. We had the savvy to manage our risks and maximize our gains by buying the crashes and HODLing the pumps while everybody else HODLed the crashes and bought into the pumps.

Some of you may have the urge to trade your crypto to institutional investors and the public in exchange for more of your government's money.

That time will come. Now is not that time.

On November 1, 2020, bear market bitcoin buyers held 39% of its total market value. In other words, 39% of the market sat in the wallets of people who bought bitcoin from 2017 to 2019.

Today, only 25% remains in their hands.

Over the same timespan, the portion held by new market entrants went from 58% to 67% and the share held by people who bought before 2017 doubled.

What does this mean?

More OGs are stacking sats as bitcoin flees from the people who have propped up the market for the past three years.

When you sold the September crash because you thought everything was going lower, who did you think was on the other end of that deal? When you took profits at $20k, who do you think gave you those profits?

Either somebody who has more faith in this market than you do, or somebody who has no interest in bitcoin and only wants to make money on "the fastest horse," as investing legend Paul Tudor Jones said.

As long as we and the OGs stay committed to cryptocurrency, this market will keep going up.

We will not have to stress about any crashes because we will already be way up on our investment. We will not have to trade in and out of the market because we got in so early, we can let everybody else push up the value of our crypto for us.

We already put in the hard work. Now it's everybody else's turn.

Today, bitcoin's price can go as low as $7,600 and as high as $80,000 and still hold its long-term, multiyear trend of rising prices (with lots of boom/bust cycles along the way). The total altcoin market could drop by 50% and still continue its upward trajectory.

As the market continues to rise, those numbers will rise, too.

Smart money always wins. If prices keep going up, we grow our wealth. If prices crash, we buy more at a discount.

With history as our guide, if the previous four market cycles play out the same way this fifth time around, we will eventually run out of people who have faith in the market.

OGs will see bitcoin's price go so high, they will not be able to sit on their gains any longer. They will feel compelled to cash out. Talk to any OG who lived through the 2017 bull run, they'll tell you the same thing.

As soon as the OGs leave, speculators will follow. Why stick around after you've made your money? Why buy when the market's crashing?

As always, altcoins will follow bitcoin.

Once the true believers and speculators leave, the market will crash. New money will get spooked.

And then the next cycle will begin.

I suspect we're a long way from that. With every crash that recovers, more people begin to believe in this asset class. With every altcoin project that weathers those inevitable, brutal 50% dumps, more people begin to think "maybe there's something there."

And for a small amount of risk, we get to benefit from all of that.

Prepare for the post-COVID-19 boom (maybe?)

Looking at the bigger picture, we still have a delicate global economic and financial environment.

That will change, too.

Within months, we will have enough people vaccinated to turn COVID-19 from a public health emergency into a communicable disease that sometimes kills people (like many other diseases).

You can bet a lot of people will refuse to take the vaccine. Their actions probably won't keep us from defeating COVID-19. Because the vaccines are so good, we might need as few as 2/3 of the population to get vaccinated. That's a realistic goal.

Once we tamp down on COVID-19, the world's economies will re-open. Supply chains will get fixed. Travel and service businesses will recover, and we will have generally more economic activity—as well as a shitload of cheap money sloshing around the world's financial markets.

You will almost certainly see profits, wages, asset values, and everything else go up. Not immediately and not obviously, but in many ways over a long period of time.

That doesn't mean we will see prosperity. We still have massive economic problems and fragile economies, not to mention social problems and growing financial inequality. I'm happy to see my property values go up—but so will my taxes, expenses, and everything else.

Already, we can see a reversal in the velocity of money, a measure of how fast people spent their cash. The faster they spend it, the faster it moves through the economy, the more wealth it creates.

Look at the velocity of money in the U.S., a proxy for the rest of the world's economies:

As you can see from looking at the right side of that chart, velocity fell like crazy from fall 2019 to summer 2020. Now it's turning up.

Sure, it could go down again, but it can't get much lower.

Once this trend reverses, more money will flow from one person to another.

Ultimately, that money will end up where it always does: in the hands of Wall Street, corporate treasurers, landlords, rich people, banks, and business leaders.

Some of the money will go back into the real economy as growth, development, payments to workers and suppliers, and general everyday purchases.

Some of the money will go into the financial markets.

Meanwhile, the world's central banks will happily keep interest rates artificially low for the foreseeable future. They've already said they will.

In this post-COVID world where cheap money abounds, you might get a bunch of people who look around, see money flowing to rich people and asset holders, and get pissed off. Then they'll see crypto prices booming and zooming, feel the emotional tug of free, open, permissionless networks, and want to use those networks to get rich—just like the elites that use the traditional financial system to do the same thing.

They may see it as the last, best chance to stick it to "the man."

Crypto is the ultimate "fuck you" money.

Altseason Cometh

If you think this money will only flow into bitcoin, you missed the story of the last two years.

Wall Street may now dominate bitcoin, but most of their products are inaccessible to people who don't have investment accounts.

Coinbase and Kraken are accessible to everybody—and they have altcoins.

The past two years have seen more and more money flow in and out of the altcoin market. Bitcoin's dominance goes up and down but has continually weakened for a year and a half. Ethereum finally produced a product that has some mainstream utility (DeFi) and many altcoins have proven their resilience and use cases. New projects proliferate and some old ones keep getting better.

This momentum has built slowly, constantly, for months and months, along with new innovations in token design, blockchain technology, U/X, off-chain data connections, and decentralized apps.

All without the benefit of Wall Street's on-ramps and institutional investors.

Now Bitwise BITW, 3iQ's ETH fund, Grayscale's Ethereum Trust, and smaller providers give large investors and financial advisors exposure to altcoins as part of a managed investment portfolio. They're easy, regulated, and free of operational and legal risks.

You can bet we'll see more altcoins get the same treatment once they grow large enough to facilitate big movements of institutional money in and out of their networks.

Once that money goes into alts, it will make bitcoin's two-month pump seem like the opening scene of a Hallmark movie.

That time will come. Get ready now so you can make the most of it when it does.

But not every project will win

Altcoins are great, but there are almost 8,000 of them.

At least 700 have legit teams, momentum, enthusiasm, and use cases that matter. Probably over 1,000 do.

Lots of great projects, awesome tech, bold visions, and strong communities (some more so than others).

Most of them will die.

Your goal can't be to put money into only the ones that see their tokens go up and none of the ones that fail. That's insane. Nobody can do that. Not even Teeka Tiwari, and certainly not that guy selling you a super-secret altcoin strategy or VIP trading service for $2,500 per year.

And if you're trying to flip alts for bitcoin or cash, you'd better know what you're doing. This is not the time or market to start playing day trader.

I prefer to find a few big winners and let them run. That means looking for smaller altcoins or big altcoins with massive potential.

Consider this analogy.

In baseball, the best-paid hitters get on base 25% of the time and strike out more than average.

If you don't know how to play baseball, you might that's odd.

Isn't the point to get on base? I mean, it's called *base*ball, right? Why pay top dollar for players who don't do that very well?

Because the point of the game is *not* to get on base. The point is to score runs.

There's no better way to accomplish that goal than to hit a home run.

For that reason, players that can hit a lot of home runs matter more than players who hit a bunch of singles and get stranded on second base.

Likewise, if you come into the market expecting every altcoin will win or give you 1,000% returns *tomorrow* (or ever), you will always be disappointed in the results. Even if you're paying $2,000 or $5,000 a year to a guy who promises you'll get 1,000% returns or he'll give you a second year's subscription for free.

The best advice I've gotten?

Think about altcoins like an early-stage investor or VC fund would.

You only need a few winners to make a huge return. In fact, the rest can go to zero and you'll still come out ahead.

That means being selective in your choices and putting money into many projects.

Look at the math.

Imagine you put $10 into ten altcoins. They're all listed on Coinbase and somebody you know tweeted about them. A few people wrote reviews about them, too. Maybe you saw some good things about them on Reddit or YouTube, or somebody mentioned them in your Telegram group. You don't know anybody on the team or connected to it, never tried the products, services, or dapps that go along with the token, and won't move your tokens off the exchange you bought them on.

If all those altcoins do 10x, you get 900% returns.

Insane gains. Incredible stuff. In any other market, you'd be a hero, legend, mythical God, etc.

Now imagine you put that money into a different 10 altcoins. They're all legit but you've never heard of half of them. To buy their tokens, you need to use obscure exchanges or Uniswap. They don't seem to have much hype. They're all fairly small and most of them are still in beta or not quite finished the main components of their network. The guy who told you about them says you should keep them off the exchanges, in private wallets that are sometimes hard to use.

By the end of this bull run, five will die. Three will stay the same price. One will do 10x. One will do 200x.

What's your return?

2,030%

Your portfolio more than doubled the returns of the guy who got those insane, seemingly impossible 1,000% windfalls on each of his altcoins.

That's how I like to play this market. I want home runs, not singles.

Along the way, we will hit some doubles and triples. In the end, we will beat the overall market by a big margin—even if most of our projects fail (which they hopefully won't).

I know many people will look at my list and those of other good analysts, see a few home runs and some strikeouts, and think I'm an idiot who got lucky a few times. And God forbid my latest recommendation doesn't do 10x and all-time highs by Christmas, otherwise it's a shitcoin and I'm a swindler.

Those same people will FOMO into the latest coin that's getting hyped on YouTube or posted on their favorite social media site. Meanwhile, my portfolio will keep growing without you ever needing to check a price chart.

You win when you get in before everybody else does

Crypto is an insider's game. You will always have a disadvantage. By the time you hear about a project, somebody else got the best opportunity to buy.

Worse, if you spend too much time on Twitter, you will always feel like you missed "the next big thing" because, out of 7,000 cryptos, all the attention that day went to that ONE altcoin that pumped and not the 6,999 other great projects that didn't. Or, when that one legit alt drops 50% in a week, everybody dismisses it as a crappy project.

At this moment, with so much to look forward to, you can't ever lose a moment's sleep thinking about a 50% drop or chasing after a 300% pump. Good projects have lots of room to run, whether or not their prices went up or down this week. Opportunities abound.

You need to get in before everybody else does. If your crypto goes up just 100% before the rest of the world finds out about it, you turn a 100x gain into a 200x gain, just by being early.

In 2017, I bought XRP at $.22, sold at $3, and felt like a genius. I didn't know XRP had already done 4,000% gains before its 15x super-pump.

No complaints about a 15x, but it would've been nice to have gotten in sooner, right?

Here's another example.

One of the research services I subscribe to mentioned one of my recommendations in a blurb for its subscribers. Here's what it wrote:

Binance Lists [my recommendation]

We picked up Binance's listing announcement for [my recommendation] on August 12th, alerting users as soon as the blog post was published on Binance's website.

Its price more than doubled in the 2.5 hours following the alert.

Note: we also notified users of the OKEx listing several hours earlier, which proved to be a solid entry point to capture short-term gains.

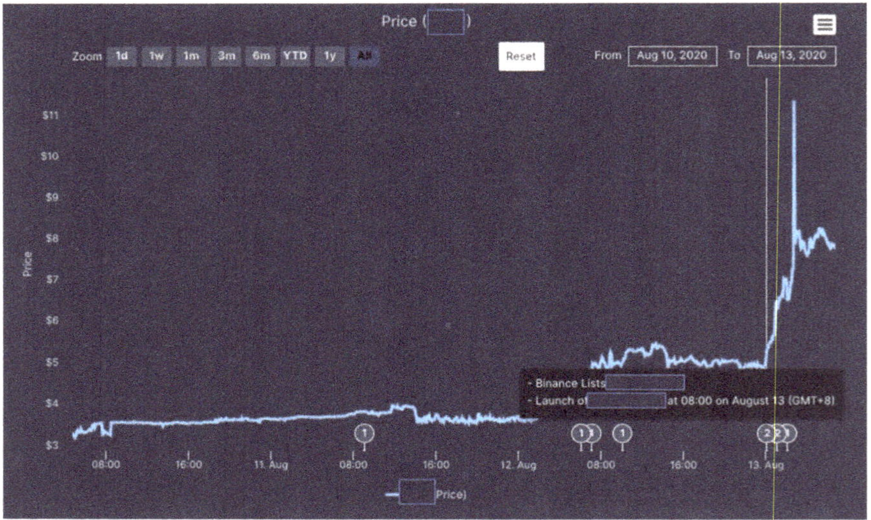

In June, I recommended this same project at $1.35. You would already have had 2.5x gains *before* this service even alerted its subscribers.

If you bought this altcoin when this other service recommended it, you would be down about 20% right now, assuming you didn't sell (btw they gave no sell alert).

If you bought this altcoin when I recommended it, you'd be up 150% right now.

Same great project, same upside, different results, simply because I got in and then waited for the price to go up, while these guys waited for the price to go up and then got in.

It's all good. This project is one of my favorites. You'll be alright in the end.

But wouldn't you have liked to be up 150% instead of down 20% right now?

Past performance . . .

Does that mean I have a magic touch?

No, but I try to find really strong projects that are far smaller than their intended use and get into them before everybody else does. That means a few whiffs, or maybe many whiffs. You can't hit home runs if you're afraid to strike out.

So far, my recommendations have outpaced the overall altcoin market. That means getting in early, sometimes months early, averaging in, staking where possible, letting the team do its work, letting the community grow around the project, and waiting for everything to work out in our favor. Or, using their tokens, if it's more than simply a financial investment.

Boring?

Maybe. Depending on what day you look (sometimes what *hour* you look), my recommendations have outperformed the market by 32-60% since March.

It's hard to get precise numbers because the market is so volatile, prices change a lot very quickly, but whether it's 32% or 60% or something else at the exact moment you check, it's great performance.

Those gains will compound over time, and if I get better at what I'm doing, my results will get better, too.

Can I guarantee that?

No. My future recommendations could do much better or much worse. This is the riskiest of risky markets, incredibly volatile, and totally speculative. Nobody can guarantee anything.

I can only promise to take the same approach that led to those earlier gains and hope the market reacts the same way it always has in the past.

You can do this!

While I'm grateful you find my content interesting and it's nice that you appreciate my thoughts, please always have faith in yourself. This market is easy if you want it to be.

You already made the great choice to enter this market now. Trust that you'll make more great choices as everything goes up.

We're early. We don't need to worry about missing the sub-$20,000 bitcoin (we just might get it again). We don't need to stress about an altcoin that drops 50% the day after we bought it. We don't need to sell after a 2x pump. A 25% swing doesn't matter yet.

For those who just arrived, we could see prices drop a lot, quickly, soon. Or go up a bit more, then crash. Or maybe even rise sharply, quickly, before falling again. Or go sideways or slightly down for a while (but most likely, crash).

If you can wait for those awesome buying opportunities that I talk about, it'll be worth the wait. But it's not worth stressing over.

If you feel the urge to buy now, DO IT.

Just don't put too much money in. Make sure you keep some fresh cash or cheap credit handy. When prices go down, they will not likely go much lower for much longer and will very likely go higher forever.

Throughout bitcoin's twelve years of history and the short history we have for altcoins, we see the same pattern over and over again: big moves up, big moves down. The bigger the move up, the bigger the move down.

That's just how markets work. It's not different because institutions have entered or because retail has started to tip-toe back in. These patterns play out over months and years, not days and weeks.

And they will always happen because they reflect human nature. Bitcoin doesn't buy and sell itself. Humans do.

Human nature never changes.

We're at that moment when everybody else will start to see what we've seen all along. It may take weeks or months to realize that shift, but it will happen.

Get ready to make the most of it.

Happy New Year. Relax and enjoy the ride!

www.ingramcontent.com/pod-product-compliance
Lightning Source LLC
Chambersburg PA
CBHW040209080726
47599CB00049B/1610